Style

Style A Pragmatic Approach

SECOND EDITION

Peter Richardson
Public Policy Institute of California

Longman

New York   San Francisco   Boston
London   Toronto   Sydney   Tokyo   Singapore   Madrid
Mexico City   Munich   Paris   Cape Town   Hong Kong   Montreal

Editor-in-Chief: Joe Opiela
Vice President: Eben Ludlow
Marketing Manager: Christopher Bennem
Senior Production Manager: Valerie Zaborski
Project Coordination and Electronic Page Makeup:
    Elm Street Publishing Services, Inc.
Cover Designer/Manager: Nancy Danahy
Print Buyer: Al Dorsey
Printer and Binder: R. R. Donnelley & Sons Company/
    Harrisonburg
Cover Printer: Phoenix Color Corp.

For permission to use copyrighted material, grateful
acknowledgment is made to the copyright holders on page 109,
which is hereby made part of this copyright page.

Library of Congress Cataloging-in-Publication Data
Richardson, Peter
    Style : a pragmatic approach / Peter Richardson.— 2nd ed.
      p.   cm.
    Includes index.
    ISBN 0-205-32108-9 (alk. paper)
    1. English language—Rhetoric. 2. English language—Style.
3. College readers. 4. Report writing. I. Title.
PE1421 .R53 2002
808'.042—dc21

                                         00-067837

Please visit our website at http://www.ablongman.com

ISBN 0-205-32108-9

1 2 3 4 5 6 7 8 9 10—DOH—04 03 02 01

Contents

Preface   ix

Chapter **1**

Writing and Conversation   1

What Speakers Know About Language   1

Applying Conversational Guidelines   2

Preconceptions About Style   4

Practical Style in the Real and Virtual World   5
▪ *Exercise 1.1*   5

Chapter **2**

Finding the Action   7

Choosing a Verb   7
▪ *Exercise 2.1*   9

Chapter **3**

Focusing the Action   11

Transitive and Intransitive Verbs   11
▪ *Exercise 3.1*   12

Complements, Modifiers, and Style   12
▪ *Exercise 3.2*   16
▪ *Exercise 3.3*   16
▪ *Exercise 3.4*   17

Chapter **4**

Staging the Characters 19

Recognizing Your Options 19

Active and Passive Voice 19

Exercise 4.1 21

Voice and Revision 21

Verb Selection Revisited 25

Exercise 4.2 25

Choosing Pronouns 26

Exercise 4.3 28

Chapter **5**

Revising for Precision 29

Identifying Problems 29

Exercise 5.1 30

Throat-Clearing 30

Overstating the Claim 31

Exercise 5.2 32

Smothering the Claim 33

Exercise 5.3 34

Chapter **6**

Making Connections 37

Speaking Versus Writing 37

The Anti-Paragraph 38

New and Given Information 39

Nominalization 41

KONAJU
BARIMA

■ *Exercise 6.1* 42

Antecedents 42
■ *Exercise 6.2* 44

Transitions 44
■ *Exercise 6.3* 46

Chapter 7

Mixing It Up 47

Rhythm, Sound, and Emphasis 47
■ *Exercise 7.1* 49

Strong Endings 50
■ *Exercise 7.2* 52

Chapter 8

Saying What You Mean 55

Some Useful Routines 55
Slowing Down 56
Developing Your Ideas 58
■ *Exercise 8.1* 59

Exploring Your Own Metaphors 60
■ *Exercise 8.2* 62

Readings 63

Personal Ads 64

Francis-Noël Thomas and Mark Turner, *Clear and Simple as the Truth* 67

Peter Brown, *The Body and Society* 70

Margaret Atwood, "The Female Body"   73

Richard Rorty, "The Intellectuals
and the Poor"   77

William Ian Miller, "Near Misses"   82

Paul Fussell, "The Boy Scout Handbook"   87

Carol J. Clover, "Men, Women, and
Chainsaws"   93

Sample Answers to Selected Exercises   97

Glossary of Terms   101

Credits   109

Index   111

Preface

The first edition of this book grew out of a few suspicions bordering on convictions. I suspected, for example, that my students already knew the most useful guidelines for stylistic revision in the same way they already knew, but couldn't always formalize, the grammatical principles of their spoken language. This much I gathered from their everyday conversations, which were organized by these same guidelines. I suspected, too, that most of my students had trouble adapting their knowledge to the demands of a particular and highly specialized technology: not the personal computer or the Internet, but the deceptively familiar technology of alphabetic literacy.

Since the publication of the first edition, many of these suspicions have become full-fledged convictions. I believe even more deeply now that the basic principles of a mature practical style are the same ones that guide our conversations. I'm also convinced that we take alphabetic literacy too much for granted. Because most of us don't study literacy historically or cross-culturally, we usually fail to see how complex, economical, and powerful it really is. Because alphabetic literacy is so familiar, we usually fail to acknowledge its artificiality as well. Compared to talking, writing is utterly unnatural. Almost everyone learns to speak without special effort, but learning to write takes years of formal instruction. Learning to write well demands even more time and effort.

So why should anyone bother to master this unnatural technology? The short answer is that in our culture, good writing matters more than we think. We rely on it to make things happen in school, at work, in our communities, and in our personal lives. When we write well, we're better at making those things happen. We may want to write fluently for other reasons, not the least of which is that it's satisfying to express ourselves clearly and well. But whatever our motives may be, we benefit from seeing our writing as something that can be shaped, polished, and improved.

This book will help you improve your writing by relating it to more familiar modes of communication, especially conversation, with which it has a great deal in common. For example, both speakers and writers often face a practical question: "Given that I want to bring about such-and-such result, what's the best way to accomplish this by using language?" Hearers and readers face a similar question: "Given that she said such–and–such, what did she mean for me to understand by that?" These questions are at the heart of pragmatics, a branch of linguistics that studies how we do things with words. Beginning with H. P. Grice, scholars in this field have noted that these questions presuppose a great deal of implicit cooperation. For a variety of reasons, this cooperation is even more crucial for writers and readers than it is for speakers and hearers. By focusing on the kinship between speech and writing and then accommodating their differences, this book applies what we know about pragmatics to the writing process in general and stylistic revision in particular.

This pragmatic approach to stylistic revision has certain advantages. One is that we don't have to learn any new "rules" or basic principles of writing. If we know how to conduct a conversation, we already know the key principles. Instead of mastering new concepts, our challenge as writers is to adapt our linguistic knowledge and social experience to the demands of written communication. To encourage this sort of adaptation, many recent textbooks use everyday conversation as a paradigm for "getting started." The main idea is to jumpstart the writing process by thinking of it as a conversation. Although I favor this approach, the similarities between speech and writing are more fruitful than most of these textbooks suggest. If we use the same guidelines to organize our conversations and our writing, these guidelines should be useful at the final stages of revision too. And indeed they are.

The pragmatic approach to stylistic revision also simplifies revision strategies. Whereas some style textbooks offer long lists of unrelated commandments—"Avoid mixed metaphors," "Never end a sentence with a preposition," "Place a free element emphatically"—this book focuses on a few general guidelines and how to apply them to specific stylistic decisions. Again, there's nothing inherently wrong with the commandments, but a pragmatic approach has several advantages over them. First, the commandments themselves are difficult to understand or apply when they're separated from the basic guidelines that motivate them. Second, the truly useful commandments can usually be derived from these guidelines anyway. Third, and perhaps most importantly, any list of stylistic commandments, no matter how sensible, creates the false impression that the writer's job is to memorize the commandments and follow them slavishly. It may seem like a fine distinction, but there's a big difference between following a "rule" whose origin is a mystery to you and applying a guideline that issues naturally from your daily experience. Even when the suggestions and routines offered in this book are identical to the commandments offered elsewhere, deriving them from the conversational guidelines will give you a better sense of where they come from, why they're useful, and how to apply them to your stylistic decisions.

I place the word *rule* in quotation marks above to maintain an important distinction. In my experience, students waste their time searching for rules when what they really need are basic strategies for recognizing their options and making better decisions. (If these strategies are grounded in a useful theory of language, so much the better.) We might compare the distinction between rules and strategies to a similar one in sports. In basketball, there are no rules against taking every shot from 50 feet away, but no knowledgeable person would recommend that strategy. That is, we can follow all the rules of basketball perfectly and still play stupidly. Likewise, the English language has rules about where prepositions and verbs can go within a sentence, but there's no "rule" in English that prohibits us from being unclear or irrelevant or boring. Rules eliminate certain choices, but style can exist only when there's more than one acceptable way to say or do something. Improving our writing style, then, is always a matter of making better decisions between grammatically acceptable alternatives.

If we're interested in what we accomplish by writing, these stylistic decisions are especially important. Whatever a fluent essay and its awkward counterpart share in the way of content, their effects are bound to be very different, if only because the fluent version will be read while the clumsy one will be put aside. By focusing on stylistic revision, we're reducing the gap between what most writers produce and what most audiences are willing to read. If you watch the way people actually read, you will know that this gap is by no means negligible.

Like its predecessor, this book is meant for writing classes of all kinds, including first-year composition. In lower-division classes, I have found it useful to read one chapter every other week and use it as a starting point for a one-period, in-class style workshop. Normally we blend exercises from the book with examples drawn from student drafts and other writing assignments. In advanced courses, I have used the book as a primary text and made more use of the anthology. Once again, the anthology selections are drawn from various discourses and disciplines. This edition includes passages from Francis-Noël Thomas and Mark Turner's *Clear and Simple as the Truth: Writing Classic Prose*, Carol J. Clover's "Men, Women, and Chainsaws: Gender in the Modern Horror Film," and William Ian Miller's "Near Misses." The first of these additions reflects my respect for Thomas and Turner's discussion of classic prose as well as their own lucid style. Carol Clover's essay on gender in the modern horror film is a model of academic writing, and Miller's essay is remarkably honest, unpredictable, and accessible to generally educated audiences. In this sense, it resembles Paul Fussell's essay and the excerpt from Richard Rorty's speech, both of which I have retained from the first edition. I have also kept the pieces by Margaret Atwood and Peter Brown. Each is provocative in its own way, and taken together, they make for interesting stylistic and topical comparisons.

Also like its precursor, this edition owes a great deal to my students, teachers, colleagues, and reviewers. I am especially grateful for the thoughtful responses and helpful suggestions from Susan R. Blau, Boston University; Douglas Downs, University of Utah; Donald C. Freeman, University of Southern California; Rebecca Moore Howard, Syracuse University; Alison Russell, Xavier University; and Mark Turner, University of Maryland. My gratitude to the reviewers of the first edition—Mary Blockley, University of Texas; Robert Funk, Eastern Illinois University; and William J. Vande Kopple, Calvin College—is undiminished. Phil Leininger, my friend and former colleague at Harper & Row, encouraged me to study at Berkeley and later to write this book. Julian Boyd, Don McQuade, and Jack Niles nurtured my interest in language and style, as did Suzanne Fleischman before her recent and untimely death. I thank them once again for their guidance and generosity.

My debts to Paul Grice, Martha Kolln, Mark Johnson, George Lakoff, Richard Lanham, Geoffrey Leech, Deborah Schiffrin, John Searle, Michael Short, William Strunk, Jr., Francis-Noël Thomas, Mark Turner, Joseph Williams, and William Zinsser will be obvious to those who have benefited from their work on style, pragmatics, and metaphor as much as I have. More recently, my work at the Public Policy Institute of California in San Francisco has allowed me to test and refine the ideas presented in this book. Among my many teachers at PPIC, Joyce Peterson and Gary Bjork have been especially helpful. More than anyone I've worked with, they lead their professional lives according to Wittgenstein's maxim that whatever can be said can be said clearly. Once again I thank my editor, Eben Ludlow, for his help in launching and guiding this effort, and Grace Trudo for her able assistance.

Since the appearance of the first edition, my daughters, Ashley and Mary, have become readers and writers in their own right. Their adventures in literacy have added an important dimension to my own. I dedicate this book to them.

1

Writing and Conversation

What Speakers Know About Language

Even if you've never studied it much, you know a lot about language. For example, you know how to take turns in a conversation. You know when other speakers are being sincere, sarcastic, or playful. You know when an exchange is coming to an end and what to do about it. In short, you're familiar with the moves and countermoves of conversation. Although this knowledge may seem basic to you now, it's the product of years of social and linguistic experience.

This knowledge enables some fairly sophisticated acts of interpretation. Suppose a co-worker brings in some cookies to your workplace, but when your break comes, all you can find is a plate with some crumbs on it. You ask the other co-workers if they ate all the cookies, and one of them says, "There weren't very many." Even though your question calls for a yes-or-no response, you quickly realize that this statement counts as an answer; the cookies are history. But how do you know? The physical and grammatical evidence (namely, the crumbs and the past tense) are major clues, of course, but your realization stems in part from your understanding of a basic conversational principle. In general, we assume that our partners are cooperating with us unless we see evidence to the contrary. In this case, you assume that your co-worker is answering your question and not just commenting on the number of cookies that were originally provided. Notice, however, that this response couldn't possibly count as an answer to your question unless you had already presumed her cooperation.

These little acts of cooperation follow certain guidelines. These aren't "rules" in the ordinary sense; they don't regulate conversations so much as they make them possible in the first place. We usually notice them only when they're ignored or flouted. Even so, they're always there, shaping and organizing our exchanges. Reviewing these guidelines is useful for two reasons. First, they help us become more aware of our own language use. Second, they help us clarify the relationship between everyday communication and a practical writing style. As basic as these guidelines are, most of us manage to ignore them in the course of writing our papers.

Applying Conversational Guidelines

At least three such guidelines apply to both conversation and written communication.

Be Relevant

If you ask me whether the cookies are gone and I reply that I like my eggs scrambled, you'll probably conclude that our exchange has misfired somehow. Usually the miscues are less obvious than this, but we all know people who seem unable to come to (or stay on) the point. Conversations with such people can be tiresome. Most readers feel the same way about rambling essays or reports; it takes too much time and energy to make sense of them, and there are more appealing things to do with one's time. Sticking to the point shows consideration for your audience and greatly improves your chances of rhetorical success.

Measure the Information

If you ask me whether any cookies are left and I spend 15 minutes recounting who ate which ones, you may feel that I haven't recognized or honored the intention behind your question. Offering too much information can kill a conversation just as effectively (if not as quickly) as offering too little. In writing, too, we need to match the amount of information we offer to the demands of the situation. In general, writers need to be more explicit than speakers, who can gesture and inflect their voices to help make their points. But the basic challenges of writing resemble those of conversation; in both, the trick is to keep things moving forward without skipping anything important.

Be Clear

Clarity is a virtue in conversation, but it's crucial in written communication. Unlike speakers, writers aren't usually on the scene to answer questions or clear up misunderstandings. Instead, writers must anticipate these questions and potential misunderstandings during the writing process.

That's the ideal, anyway. In reality, we often go to great lengths to make our writing more obscure, usually by lacing it with fancy words and phrases. We do this for at least two reasons. First, it sometimes makes us sound smart or important even when we're saying something trivial. Second, an obscure style makes it easier to downplay or even conceal unpleasant facts. For example, an overblown sentence ("Third-quarter earnings experienced a temporary downward adjustment") might work better at a shareholder meeting than a more straightforward version ("Profits are down"). Although a pretentious style works well in some situations—no one would use it if it didn't—it often backfires, sometimes disastrously, in college writing. Far from making us sound smart or important, it raises questions about our credibility. Experienced readers know that this style often accompanies unclear thinking or attempts to manipulate the audience. Pretense and obscurity don't impress these readers so much as make them suspicious.

When it comes to writing, everyone is for clarity, but almost no one talks about its costs. To write clearly, we have to think carefully about our topic, pay attention to language, and anticipate our audience's responses, all of which require a good deal of mental and imaginative effort. If we decide not to make that effort, we shouldn't expect our readers to pick up the slack. We might compare this situation to planning a meal for a group of guests. One option is to place the groceries on the table and invite the guests to make something out of them. Another is to buy the groceries, prepare the ingredients, cook the meal, and serve it to our guests. Neither option is inherently right or wrong, but they shouldn't be confused. Likewise, insisting that our ideas are perfect even though our prose is unclear is like ignoring the difference between a pile of groceries and a well-prepared meal. If our writing is half-baked, we shouldn't be surprised if our readers aren't savoring it.

Clarity has a hidden cost as well. When we rid our sentences and paragraphs of vague language, we often discover our own faulty assumptions, logical fallacies, and weak transitions. This discovery can be irritating, but it can also be turned to advantage if we're willing to rethink and rewrite extensively. This sort of revision shouldn't be mistaken for decoration or ornamentation; it doesn't spruce up preexisting ideas so much as shape better ones.

As ordinary as these three guidelines are, they're surprisingly difficult to follow. At some level, we all know we should stick to the point, measure the information, and write clearly; the important question is how we can do this more consistently. This book answers that question by offering practical suggestions for stylistic revision. Most of the suggestions are specific and local, but all can be traced to the general guidelines of relevance, proportion, and clarity. These guidelines and suggestions don't exhaust the subject of style, or even the one style with which this book is concerned; but if you use them consistently and thoughtfully, your writing will be clearer, more focused, and more effective.

Preconceptions About Style

Most of us don't think about style very often, but many of us hold certain preconceptions about it. Some of us think that style means decoration or ornamentation; or that style is the slightly inferior opposite of substance; or that serious people in the real world have no time or use for it. These preconceptions aren't ridiculous so much as predictably misguided. We're taught early on to regard style as the dress of thought, as something separable from and more superficial than our best thinking. Many of us go on from there to associate style with all that is artificial and mannered.

Although this is the most prevalent conception of style, it isn't the most useful one. Given that writing gets things done at work as well as in our schools, communities, and personal lives, it makes better sense to regard fluent prose as a species of effective action. When seen this way, the stylistic choices we make while composing are best understood as necessary, significant, and indispensable parts of that action. As for serious people in the real world, they usually have time for clear, economical writing. What they don't have time for is baggy, pointless prose.

Notice that this conception of style rules out the possibility of writing with no style whatsoever. No matter how committed we are to substance, or how averse we are to artifice, we're always making stylistic decisions when we write. We may not be aware of these decisions, and we may not always make good ones, but we make them nevertheless. In this sense, a prose style is like a haircut; we can ignore our hair or cut it off completely, but we can't choose not to have a hairstyle at all. Since we must have a writing style, it makes sense to develop one that works for us.

P ractical Style in the Real and Virtual World

There are many mature prose styles, but this book concentrates on what is usually called practical style, which is characterized by some loose-knit, overlapping, and crisscrossing assumptions, goals, and general habits. When we talk about practical style in the singular, we're not attempting to define it narrowly or definitively; rather, we're trying to distinguish it from other styles with different assumptions and goals.

As the name implies, practical style helps us do things: impart information, urge a course of action, make a decision, reach a judgment, explain a process, solve a problem, and so on. At its best, practical style is lucid and even elegant, but its chief virtue is versatility. Other styles are more playful, sophisticated, sensual, or spectacular, but none is more consistently useful in our everyday lives. Practical style works especially well with college audiences, especially instructors, whose reading habits are determined by time constraints and institutional responsibilities. It would be a mistake, however, to conclude that this style has no place in the "real" (or virtual) world. Those who write for the Web, for example, often favor practical style for its clarity and economy. Whether or not readers are aware of it, they expect and value this style in a wide range of settings, especially but not only on the Internet.

Practical style is frequently underestimated because it seems to be no style at all, especially when it's working well. But this underestimation rarely persists. Readers eventually get fed up with lame writing, and most audiences are extraordinarily receptive to clear, balanced prose. As long as this is the case, practical style will be worth mastering.

E*xercise 1.1*

Read the personal ads on pages 64 and 65. How well do their authors follow the guidelines of relevance, proportion, and clarity? What happens when the authors ignore those guidelines?

2

Finding the Action

Choosing a Verb

Generating sentences isn't all that difficult; we do it every day in conversation without a second thought. The trouble comes when we have to write a hundred or so cohesive sentences and submit them to an experienced reader for evaluation. Very few of us do this every day, and doing it well requires a lot of second thoughts. Most of us break that one large writing task into a series of smaller ones by writing for a while, showing a draft to some readers, revising the draft in light of their reactions, and continuing to revise until we have something we can live with. But however we go about it, writing means making a series of decisions about the best way to present our ideas.

Whether or not we are aware of it, one of the most important decisions we make concerns the verb. Consider the following sentence:

There *is* opposition to the initiative among a majority of taxpayers.

Notice that nothing actually happens in this sentence. Part of this problem has to do with the verb, which doesn't convey a strong sense of action. If we ask where the action is, or who is doing what, the answer seems to have something to do with *opposition*. Converting that word into something more action-oriented, we get the following:

A majority of taxpayers *are opposed* to the initiative.

This sentence is a bit clearer than the original, but it still lacks a strong sense of action. If we make *oppose* the main verb and trim some other language, the result is even crisper.

Most taxpayers *oppose* the initiative.

Notice that all three sentences are grammatically correct, but the third version best satisfies our guideline of clarity. It's a bonus that this version is also the shortest; we now have more space to modify or elaborate our point or to proceed to another one. By selecting an action-oriented verb that was already hiding in the original sentence, we produced a clearer sentence with more shape and direction.

Poor verb choices often produce wordiness and unnecessary abstraction. Notice the wasted energy in the following sentence:

The function of management *is* to be a watchdog for the shareholder.

Once again we have a weak sense of action; but we also have other, more attractive options within the original sentence. By using *function* as a verb instead of a noun, we can make the same point more straightforwardly:

Management *functions* as a watchdog for the shareholder.

Although this version is more concise, it still doesn't sound right. The problem now is a mismatch between the verb and the other elements in the sentence. We don't normally say that a watchdog *functions*, though we might say that it *acts* or *serves*. Let's try one of these.

Management *acts* as a watchdog for the shareholder.

Again, this version is clearer and more concise than the original. Of course, we could go on to entertain other changes as well. We might tinker with the subject, for example, or reconsider the watchdog metaphor. How exactly is management like a watchdog, and how does this comparison help us establish our main point? But wherever we decide to end our revisions, the verb provides an excellent starting point for fixing awkward or wordy sentences.

Poor verb choices cause other problems as well. Most of the lumps in the following sentence can be traced to the verb:

The Governor *issued* an order that all state employees must follow the new procedures pertaining to travel.

In this case, the first three words of the verb phrase (*issued an order*) already suggest excess bulk. *Order* is also a verb, and we can use it that way here. Trimming some other verbiage leaves us with the following:

The Governor *ordered* all state employees to follow the new travel procedures.

Here again, the streamlining is largely a matter of finding the action and choosing a good verb.

Suitable verbs don't just roll off the keyboard at the right time. They must be selected, more or less consciously, from a wide range of possibilities. We don't stop to review these possibilities in conversation, and we may not wish to weigh the pros and cons of particular verbs even in our first drafts. As we close in on a final paper, however, it often pays to fuss over the verbs. Some writers consult a thesaurus in an effort to find just the right word. Alternatively, a good verb sometimes appears as a noun in an early draft; in that case, we can intensify the sentence and dissolve abstraction by converting the noun into a verb. However we do it, selecting verbs according to our three guidelines will sharpen our style. This sort of local revision takes time and effort, but it's the surest way to lucid, balanced prose.

Exercise 2.1

Revise the following sentences by selecting new verbs. If possible, convert an abstract noun into the main verb.

1. The diaries are a depiction of the hypocrisy of that period.
2. The memorandum contains the implication that what happened was proper.
3. His fear of failure was a hindrance in his relationship with his son.
4. This film does a successful job of documenting the excitement of a political campaign.
5. They came to the conclusion that the results were invalid.
6. The author makes a comparison between the schools of the 1940s and today's schools.
7. There is an obvious desire within her for a healthy, balanced relationship.
8. There's no necessity for the establishment of protocols for these cases.
9. There is a variation in the need for charity care across cities and states.
10. The focus of the research presented in this report is on the relationship between residents and their elected officials.

3

Focusing the Action

Transitive and Intransitive Verbs

In the previous chapter, we saw that verbs animate their sentences, and that this effect makes verb choice especially important. But verbs do more than animate sentences; they also shape them. When we choose a verb, we also choose the sentence elements that necessarily accompany it. For example, the verb *recommend* requires two additional elements to "complete" its meaning. We don't just recommend; we recommend something to someone. When we choose this verb, then, we need to make room in our sentence for a direct object (whatever is recommended) and an indirect object (whoever receives the recommendation):

> Robin recommended   *the movie*   *to Leigh*.

The elements that accompany a verb and complete its meaning are called *complements*. Verbs that require at least one complement are *transitive*; those that require no complements are said to be *intransitive*. Here are some examples of transitive and intransitive verbs. (Note: an asterisk indicates that a sentence isn't well formed.)

Transitive

> I *bought* the shoes.
>
> Chris *admired* them.
>
> Pat *persuaded* me to leave them on the porch.

11

* I bought.

* Chris admired.

* Pat persuaded.

Intransitive

The customer *laughed.*

The new business *failed.*

The owner *wept.*

[handwritten: Trans. verbs need complements]

[handwritten: Int. don't might need no pattern but don't need for a complete thought]

Of course, we can always add other elements after the verb, even an intransitive one. For example, we can say that the customer laughed at the joke, uproariously, in the showroom, after lunch, with his friends, and so on. But these extra elements aren't complements because we don't need them to express a complete thought. Instead, they're called *modifiers* because they modify, rather than complete, the meaning of the verb.

Because we often need modifiers to qualify or limit the meaning of a verb, they're an important part of good style. From a grammatical standpoint, however, modifiers are optional; we don't need them to form meaningful sentences. There are many kinds of modifiers, but for now we'll focus on modifiers as they apply to verbs. As we will see, distinguishing them from complements is a useful revision tool.

Exercise 3.1

Identify the complements in the following sentences.

1. Life in all of its complexity imitates art.
2. She endured slander and calumny over her 40-year career.
3. Did you order the tickets for the show on Friday night?
4. In a long and sometimes rambling harangue, he cited several failed policies.
5. His principal argument challenges common sense understandings of what is known to economists as the fallacy of composition.

Complements, Modifiers, and Style

Distinguishing modifiers from complements pertains to stylistic revision because modifiers, unlike complements, can be cut from wordy sentences. In many cases, we can fix a fouled-up sentence by locating the verb and its complements and then determining which modifiers can be eliminated. Of course, the fact that we can eliminate modifiers doesn't mean that we should. Sometimes a modifier is the most remarkable part of a sentence, as in the following example from F. Scott Fitzgerald's *The Great Gatsby*:

> I am still a little afraid of missing something if I forget that, as my father *snobbishly* suggested, and as I *snobbishly* repeat, a sense of fundamental decencies is parcelled out unequally at birth.

Here the modifier *snobbishly* pays its own way, so to speak. If Fitzgerald had deleted it for the sake of economy, he would have produced a much less striking sentence. Not all modifiers are so helpful, however, and the less helpful ones often cloud the main assertion. Consider the following sentence:

> Basically, the Sumerians created certain patterns and particular conventions for the making of the human image.

The verb *created* requires one complement to complete its meaning; the Sumerians created something. In this case, we have two direct objects, (*patterns* and *conventions*); but do we really need the modifiers *basically*, *certain*, and *particular*? Without them, the sentence reads as follows:

> The Sumerians created patterns and conventions for the making of the human image.

We don't seem to miss the modifiers here, and we're probably better off without them. We can always add them back for emphasis or nuance; but if the streamlined sentence will do, we may as well stick with it.

Eliminating unnecessary modifiers is an important part of stylistic revision. Notice the extra baggage in the following sentence:

> Personally, I believe that the ability to trim unnecessary or redundant modifiers improves the effectiveness of an author's writing style.

Let's start with the very first word of this example. We don't need to modify I *believe* with *personally*, as such beliefs are usually personal. Nor do we need to modify the main assertion with the disclaimer that we believe it; most readers will assume that we believe what we say. *Unnecessary* and *redundant* seem to overlap; redundant modifiers are usually unnecessary. In fact, the verb *trim* probably eliminates the need for both terms; we usually trim only what is unnecessary. Another easy inference follows from the verb choice; when we improve a writing style, we usually improve its effectiveness. Finally, an author's style is usually understood to be a writing style. Without the redundancies, and with a few other snips, the sentence reads as follows:

> Trimming modifiers improves an author's style.

We make life easier for our readers when we delete this verbiage, but there's a certain satisfaction in it for us, too. By shedding the extra weight, our sentences and paragraphs take on more shape, direction, and energy. As we will see later, this sort of revision also helps us decide where to go with the next sentence.

So far we've looked at one-word modifiers, but whole phrases can modify sentences as well. Sometimes these modifying phrases produce confusion, as in the following sentence:

> Conrad believes that the Victorian theory of work as a beneficial barrier to the dark side of human nature is inherently harmful to the human condition.

Most of us will need to read this sentence more than once to understand it. As a first step toward clarification, let's start with the main verb. *Believes* is transitive; we don't just believe, we believe something. But what does Conrad, the subject of the sentence, believe? Something about the Victorian theory of work, it seems, but things become murky after that. In this case, the problems seem to start with the long modifying phrase beginning with "as a beneficial barrier." If we bracket that modifying phrase, the main point becomes clearer:

> Conrad believes that the Victorian theory of work [as a beneficial barrier to the dark side of human nature] is harmful to the human condition.

Now let's try deleting that modifying phrase:

> Conrad believes that the Victorian theory of work is harmful to the human condition.

Now at least we have a comprehensible sentence, but our work isn't over; we still need to unpack the idea expressed in the deleted phrase. Notice, however, that burying that idea in a modifying phrase only confounds the sentence as a whole. By eliminating the phrase, we can untangle the two claims and present them sequentially. This arrangement follows our guideline of clarity more closely.

Excessive modification can even cause us to lose track of the governing verb, as in the following sentence:

> The discussion reflected a range of diverse and sometimes controversial opinions about the significance of the upcoming election, as well as a brief but informative summary of the upcoming initiatives.

The verb (*reflected*) and its first complement (*a range of opinions*) are fine. However, by the time we arrive at the second complement (*summary*), the sentence has begun to lose its focus. What exactly does it mean to say that a discussion reflects a summary? The sentence is grammatical, of course, but the verb and the complement don't make a good match, and separating them with a string of modifiers only masks the problem. By way of a remedy, we might change the verb *reflected* to *included*:

> The discussion *included* a range of diverse and sometimes controversial opinions about the significance of the upcoming election, as well as a brief but informative summary of the upcoming initiatives.

This looks to be a good solution, though we could have reconsidered the complements as well. The point is that selecting a suitable verb does little good if we saddle it with awkward complements.

These examples show that verbs, complements, and modifiers are more than grammatical categories; they're also useful revision tools. By attending to them, we can intensify the action in our writing and eliminate distracting language. It's important to remember three things: that verbs are literally where the action is; that transitive verbs need compatible complements; and that modifiers should pay their own way. Notice that these reminders flow directly from our conversational maxims of relevance, proportion, and clarity. Ill-considered modifiers tend to disfigure sentences and obscure their meaning. Because they're often irrelevant as well, eliminating them tends to sharpen our sentences and paragraphs.

Our key revision questions, then, are the following:

- Do we have the right verb?
- Are the complements compatible with it?
- Do the modifiers add anything important?

If the answer to any of these questions is no, we should keep revising our sentence until it satisfies our guidelines of clarity, proportion, and relevance.

Exercise 3.2

Review the sentences for verb-complement compatibility.

1. The seminars provide various professional and personal strategies and concepts for greater productivity and self-esteem.
2. The high school experience represents a broad range of social, academic, artistic, and athletic endeavors.
3. For these authors, history consists of the deeds of politicians and generals, and not the idea that the lives of ordinary people are important.
4. The Community Center fosters a safe, fun, and stimulating location where teenagers can meet and interact.
5. The presiding officer noted the lateness of the hour as well as the observation that she was getting tired herself.

Exercise 3.3

Review the verb choices and eliminate unnecessary modifiers.

1. It's definitely difficult to find too many similarities between James Brown and Beck.
2. The Victorian time period had a class system under which cruelty was tolerated and perpetuated.
3. Case studies of marketing mistakes provided the stimulus for a comprehensive and thorough review of competition among brewers.
4. International aid groups had a somewhat lackluster degree of success after the withdrawal of the diplomats from the capitol had occurred.
5. Both the profit status of a hospital and whether it is affiliated with or owned by a multihospital corporation may have important effects on a hospital's organization and service provision, hospital costs, access to care, and quality of care.

Exercise 3.4

Review the verb choices and modifiers and revise for economy.

It is critical that all personnel at Foothill High School be trained on the Internet provided through your Instructional Technologist at various times already this year. The reason that this is critical is because the Internet is and will be the basic avenue in which communication among staff and the providing of Instructional services will evolve. We have been given a rapidly approaching deadline that Internet training will be discontinued for the year by the district.

4

Staging the Characters

R *ecognizing Your Options*

Finding, focusing, and intensifying the action is a crucial part of stylistic revision, but how we stage the actors is just as important. As we have seen, verbs carry with them an implicit cast of characters; the verb *send,* for example, assumes a sender, a receiver, and something sent. When we write, we can feature these characters in various ways. Just as directors must decide how to stage or shoot a scene, we must decide how to connect the actors and events in our writing. These decisions will depend on what we wish to emphasize, and once again, making good decisions begins with recognizing our options.

In some situations, the event itself is more important than the actors. Scientific writing, for example, tends to stress natural events and processes rather than the scientists who observe them. In other situations, the actors themselves are vital. It may not suffice in a legal proceeding to say that a crime was committed; eventually, we may want to know who committed it. In this chapter, we'll explore strategies for making good decisions in different situations. Once again, we'll appeal to our three conversational guidelines to help us make those decisions.

A *ctive and Passive Voice*

Staging the characters, like focusing the action, involves a set of sentence-level decisions beginning with the verb. The most important of these decisions concerns *voice,* a category of the verb that frames the relationship between characters and events. English grammar has two voices: active and passive. The active voice is expressed with the simple form of the verb, as in the following examples:

ACTIVE VOICE

Chris *made* a mistake.

The party leadership *opposes* the measure.

Our hosts *entertained* us royally.

The chair *adjourned* the meeting.

The alternative is the passive voice, which combines a form of *be* with the past participle of the main verb.

PASSIVE VOICE

A mistake *was made* (by Chris).

The measure *is opposed* (by the party leadership).

We *were entertained* royally (by our hosts).

The meeting *was adjourned* (by the chair).

Notice that only transitive verbs can take the passive voice; intransitive verbs such as *weep* and *sunbathe* cannot.

Notice, too, that in the passive sentences, the source of the action (sometimes called the *agent*) isn't the grammatical subject of the sentence. When we switch from the active to the passive voice, we remove the agent from the sentence's subject slot:

Active: Leslie kissed Dana.

Passive: Dana was kissed (by Leslie).

Here the direct object in the active sentence, Dana, becomes the grammatical subject of the passive sentence. By promoting the direct object to the subject slot, the passive construction puts the original agent out of work, so to speak. In our example, we don't need to mention Leslie at all for the second sentence to be well formed. As we will see, we can use this transformation to help shape audience expectations. In contrast, the active sentences place the agent in the sentence's subject slot. As a result, there is less abstraction and room for doubt about who did what in these sentences.

There are good reasons to prefer this more straightforward arrangement. Perhaps the chief reason has to do with audience expectations. Readers expect to see major characters in the sentence's subject slot and major actions in the verb slot. We don't always have to satisfy that expectation, of course, and it often makes sense to play against it; but in most cases, a sentence with an agent in the subject slot and a verb in the active voice makes audience cooperation easier and more likely.

Exercise 4.1

Rewrite the following by switching active sentences to passive ones and vice versa.

advertising have been used w/ g. succ.
1. Politicians have used advertising with great success. *(by pol.)*
2. Ten cases of measles were reported by local parents.
3. Several arguments have been advanced by proponents of the plan.
4. The company hired 90 percent of its current work force between 1980 and 1985.
5. The charges were investigated by the committee and were found to be false.

Voice and Revision

Although we don't usually think about voice in our conversations or first drafts, we're constantly choosing between active and passive forms whenever we speak or write. Revision allows us to reconsider these decisions, and we can do so in light of our conversational guidelines. Given that passive constructions promote the direct object to subject position, we must ask whether this promotion helps us achieve relevance, proportion, and clarity.

Relevance

In most cases, audiences like to know who is doing what. For example, baseball announcers don't usually say that a home run was hit in the second inning, mostly because whoever hit the home run is usually important information. In other situations, however, the agent is irrelevant. Sticking with our baseball example, we rarely hear an announcer say that the umpire called the base runner out. No one cares about the umpire, and besides, who else would make the call? Another reason for not specifying the umpire is that doing so might divert attention from our main interest, the call itself. When agents are distracting or irrelevant, we should pass over them in silence. In such cases, the passive construction comes in handy because it either omits the agent or downplays it by placing it outside the subject slot, where readers expect to see major characters.

Speakers and writers frequently choose the passive voice because the agent is all too relevant and must therefore be concealed or downplayed. If a political leader answers allegations of misdeeds by admitting that "mistakes were made," his or her opponents are unlikely to let it go at that. Such ploys are transparent, sometimes painfully so, and they tend to alienate impartial audiences. If we hope to maintain good faith with our readers, we shouldn't manipulate voice to conceal or obscure agency when that information is relevant.

Proportion

Voice directly affects the way we measure information. As we have seen, mentioning an irrelevant agent provides too much information, while omitting a relevant one doesn't provide enough. Measuring the information, however, involves more than regulating the *quantity* of information. It also means measuring the flow and signaling the relative value of that information. Manipulating voice can help us do that. Consider the opening passage of a recent style textbook (my emphasis):

> The more student papers I read, the more I think that America's current epidemic verbal ineptitude comes on two levels, rudimentary and stylistic. The rudimentary level *is caused* by a failure to teach simple functional literacy. Students on this level make mistakes from ignorance. They don't know the rules. On the stylistic level, though, something different happens. You are not so much making "writing errors" as trying, usually with indifferent success, to imitate a predominant style, one you see all around you.

In the first sentence, the author distinguishes between rudimentary and stylistic ineptitude. He reinforces that distinction by beginning the second sentence with one of those terms. Notice that the author, who elsewhere advises his readers to avoid the passive voice, uses a passive construction in the second sentence of his opening paragraph. He has at least one good reason for doing so. By using the passive construction here, he promotes a key term to the subject slot, where it receives more attention than if he had buried it in the middle of the sentence.

Now consider the alternative:

> The more student papers I read, the more I think that America's current epidemic verbal ineptitude comes on two levels, rudimentary and stylistic. A failure to teach simple functional literacy *causes* the rudimentary level. Students on this level make mistakes from ignorance.

This formulation gives the passage a slightly different emphasis, which now seems to fall on the teaching failure rather than the distinction between rudimentary and stylistic ineptitude. Instead of developing a key distinction, the paragraph threatens to shoot off in another direction.

In the original version, the author uses the passive voice to control what goes in the subject slot. By doing so, he maintains *topic continuity*—that is, he keeps a single topic in sharp focus throughout the paragraph. At the same time, he signals the relative importance of characters and action. Both are important parts of measuring information.

Clarity

Many teachers and authors instruct writers to avoid passive constructions altogether. The motive for this advice is clear enough; passive constructions often make sentences and paragraphs difficult to follow. Notice how the complexity and awkwardness mount in the following sequence of sentences.

> Chris promised to rewrite this sentence to eliminate the passive voice.

> A promise was made by Chris to rewrite this sentence to eliminate the passive voice.

> A promise was made by Chris that this sentence would be rewritten to eliminate the passive voice.

> A promise was made by Chris that this sentence would be rewritten so that the passive voice would be eliminated.

When a passive sentence is convoluted, overly abstract, or just plain fouled up, switching to the active voice often helps. This correlation between passive constructions and unclear sentences has prompted the standard advice about avoiding the passive voice. As we've seen, the passive voice can foul a sentence, and we must learn to recognize and correct its misuses. But we've also seen that the passive construction does valuable work, and we shouldn't hesitate to use that construction when that work needs doing. Again, no rule on this matter will help us write better prose; we can only consult our guidelines and do our best to apply them to the situation at hand.

Let's take more examples and see where the passive voice is and isn't advisable. Consider the following lead for a story on the sports page:

> Shaquille O'Neal scored 40 points and grabbed 24 rebounds as the Lakers overcame an injury to Kobe Bryant to defeat the Indiana Pacers Friday night.

Notice the straightforwardness of this formulation. Agents in the subject slot and verbs in the active voice make these sentences especially easy to follow. Now let's try this same passage in the passive voice:

> Forty points were scored and 24 rebounds were grabbed by Shaquille O'Neal and an injury to Kobe Bryant was overcome by the Lakers as the Indiana Pacers were defeated Friday night.

One good reason for preferring the original version has to do with audience expectations. Readers expect the first sentence to emphasize the players, not disembodied statistics. In this case, then, the active voice is preferable to the passive.

Now let's try a sentence from the real estate portion of the newspaper:

> The Gresham house, which was built in 1977, was designed to save energy and to achieve harmony with the landscape. It has been featured in *Better Homes and Gardens* and *Architectural Digest*.

Here the goal is to generate interest in a house, and the author must make decisions about emphasis accordingly. Switching to the active voice in the first sentence would mean specifying the house's builder and designer, which could take the spotlight off the house itself. Likewise, the active voice in the second sentence would put the magazines in the subject slot. Is this the emphasis we want? Let's pose this question against the larger backdrop of our three guidelines. Do these changes make these sentences clearer, more measured, or more relevant to the topic at hand? Probably not. Unless choosing these other subjects helps us achieve our goal of generating interest in the house, we're better off keeping the focus as it is.

V *erb Selection Revisited*

So far we have discussed voice as if our verb choices were final. Frequently, however, we can avoid difficult decisions about voice by choosing new verbs. Notice the string of passive constructions in the following passage:

> The last Muslims were driven from Spain in 1492, but most of the country had been won back to Christianity even before. The kingdom of Morocco, though firmly Islamic, was never regained as a unified Mediterranean state. Eventually the Turkish caliphate was toppled by a brutal invasion of Mongol troops in 1258. From that point until after World War II, most Arabs were governed by foreigners.

This paragraph does at least two things well; it keeps the spotlight on Muslims and their institutions, and no sentence is especially unclear. Even so, the sheer number of passive constructions drains the passage of vitality. We can reverse this effect by choosing new verbs in the active voice:

> The last Muslims *retreated* from Spain in 1492, but most of this country had been won back to Christianity even before. The kingdom of Morocco, though firmly Islamic, was never regained as a unified Mediterranean state. Eventually the Turkish caliphate *fell* before a brutal invasion of Mongol troops in 1258. From that point until after World War II, most Arabs were governed by foreigners.

These changes break up the monotony of the passive constructions without sacrificing the topic continuity of the original paragraph. By reconsidering our verb choices, then, we can put agents back in the subject slot and still maintain topic continuity.

E*xercise 4.2*

Review the voice decisions in the following passages and revise where necessary. make sense

1. Science is made by human beings, a self-evident fact that is far too often forgotten. If that fact is recalled here, it is in the hope of reducing the gap between two cultures, the humanities and science. Science is based on experiments; its results are attained by talks among those who work in it and consult one another about their interpretation of these experiments.

2. These achievements must be accorded second place by the historian in favor of an ideological struggle. Out of a far-reaching controversy

on the nature of the right order to be established in the world, the pattern of civilization of the following centuries was to emerge. These years were dominated by an attempt at world revolution that influenced in highly effective ways the other aspects of social change. It seems that it was almost necessary that the social order be shaken to its foundations by a revolutionary onslaught, so that the new political, economic, and intellectual forces could be given the opportunity to develop in the face of the old institutions and ideas.

3. The argument that all the wrong people are helped by such public spending is familiar from the Marxist tradition, and it comes as something of a surprise to encounter so "subversive" a reasoning among advocates of the free enterprise system. But this is not the first time that strange bedfellows were made by shared hatreds. The hatred that is shared in this case is directed against attempts to re-form some unfortunate or unjust features of the capitalist system through public intervention and programs. On the Far Left, such programs are criticized because it is feared that any success they might have would reduce revolutionary zeal. On the Right, they are subjected to criticism and mockery because any intervention of the state is considered noxious or futile interference with a system that is supposed to be self-equilibrating.

C *hoosing Pronouns*

Another set of staging decisions involves the use of pronouns: *he, she, it, we,* and so on. Here again, stylistic decisions aren't made by appeal to rules but rather to practical guidelines. Although pronouns and nouns must agree in number and gender, there is no rule, for example, that banishes first-person pronouns (*I, we*) from academic writing. As the anthology selections in this book show, many academic writers use these pronouns without hesitation; in some cases, this habit seems to be part of their rhetorical strategy. At the same time, other writers believe that avoiding these pronouns makes their prose more objective and authoritative and less self-important and presumptuous. This belief often leads to the generous use of passive constructions, which keep these pronouns out of the subject position (see the first selection of Exercise 4.2). Notice, however, that the chief consideration for both sorts of writers isn't a rule but rather a set of calculations about likely audience reactions.

Pronouns present us with unusual stylistic decisions, mostly because the English pronoun system is unusual. Unlike other European languages (or even earlier stages of English), Modern English doesn't assign a grammatical gender to each noun. It does, however, assign a gender to its singular pronouns. As a result, we must choose a grammatical gender in sentences like the following:

Each writer must make this decision for (himself, herself). If (he, she) considers it significant, then (he, she) must somehow signal that significance to (his, her) readers.

Let's suppose that it doesn't matter whether our imagined writer in this sentence is a male or female. On one hand, choosing a masculine or feminine pronoun might distract readers from the main point about writers and decision-making. On the other, including both pronouns adds unnecessary complexity.

In the past, many writers solved this problem by consistently choosing masculine pronouns, even when these pronouns were supposed to refer to men and women. Some writers still prefer this solution, but they risk excluding, alienating, or even insulting large parts of their readership by doing so. Sensitive to that kind of failure, other writers try to soft-pedal the decision in the following way:

Each writer must make this decision for themselves.

This solution violates the grammatical rule that pronouns and nouns should agree in number: *Each writer* is singular, *themselves* is plural. The urge to switch to the plural is helpful, however, in part because plural pronouns, unlike singular ones, are not marked for gender. By changing the noun and pronoun to a plural form, we can take the focus off men and women and emphasize writers and their decisions:

Writers must make this decision for themselves.

This version may sacrifice specificity—the original puts the spotlight on the individual writer, not writers as a group—but it approximates the original point without breaking a grammatical rule or mismeasuring the information.

At least two other options exist. Some writers alternate, more or less randomly, between masculine and feminine pronouns. We can also recast the sentence to eliminate any such decision:

Each writer must make this decision.

As a writer, one must make this decision for oneself.

Again, the emphasis differs slightly in both cases, but depending on the context, one of these sentences might work well. As this discussion indicates, pronoun selection problems don't always have elegant or universal solutions, but it helps to know what our options are.

Exercise 4.3

Review the pronoun choices and revise where necessary.

1. In such cases, the defendant's right to remain silent cannot be abridged, even if their silence endangers another officer.

2. When you're dealing with that kind of attorney, you have to be careful not to arouse her suspicions.

3. This rhetorical strategy flatters the reader by making him part of the solution to the problem under consideration.

Revising for Precision

I dentifying Problems

The English language provides us with many devices for hedging our assertions. We hear this sort of hedging frequently in conversation: *maybe, sorta, I guess, kinda*, and so on. We even have a set of auxiliary or helping verbs we can use for a similar purpose. When we say, for example, "It *may* rain tomorrow," we're softening the prediction that it will rain. Such softening is indispensable, if only because some predictions and assertions require this sort of qualification. Stylistic problems arise, however, when our hedging doesn't add precision so much as disguise imprecise thinking and writing. This chapter identifies and addresses some of these problems. In particular, it focuses on words and phrases that frequently flag weak points in our thinking and expression. Instead of concealing these weak points more artfully, our goal will be to strengthen them through revision.

When we sit down to write a paper, most of us avoid the informal hedging that abounds in conversation. We don't write *sorta* or *kinda like* in an essay or report, even if we use these phrases in our everyday exchanges. One reason we avoid these phrases has to do with audience expectations. We sense that college readers expect more formality, and that challenging this expectation will be an uphill climb to the bottom. Informality, however, is only one problem associated with these colloquialisms; another is that they're notoriously vague. Many writers solve the informality problem by replacing the colloquialisms with fancier but equally imprecise substitutes. Consider the following "translations" from informal to formal diction:

INFORMAL	FORMAL
The judge was *sorta* angry.	The judge was *somewhat* angry.
The judge was *really* angry.	The judge was *extremely* angry.

However elevated these translations sound, they still suggest the need for more revision. If a word or phrase requires a *somewhat*, *very*, or *extremely* to modify it, there's a good chance that another word or phrase will work better. For example, *somewhat angry* can be replaced with *irritated* or *annoyed*. Likewise, *irate, furious, livid*, or *enraged* can substitute for *extremely angry*. Notice that these adjectives are briefer, more specific, and more evocative than the phrases they replace. Of course, the best word won't always spring immediately to mind; but once again, revision allows us the chance to review our choices, consult a thesaurus, or look up a word in the dictionary.

Exercise 5.1

Replace the underlined phrase with a single word. Consult a thesaurus or dictionary if necessary.

1. In its day, this novel was considered <u>somewhat obscene.</u> *indecent*
2. The teacher was <u>to a certain extent happy</u> with the class's performance. *satisfied*
3. Although she scandalized most critics, audiences across the country found her <u>extremely humorous.</u> *interesting*
4. There was something <u>rather vulgar</u> about the circus-like atmosphere of the trial. *obscene*
5. The witness appeared to be <u>totally mixed up</u> by the line of questioning. *confused*

Throat-Clearing

As we saw in an earlier chapter, another way to hedge claims is to preface them with reminders that they reflect our opinions, beliefs, or hopes.

> I *think that* if this character were a woman in society today, she would be very credible. *I feel that* she definitely possesses authority and *I hope that* this paper has shown that.

> *It is my belief that* Johnson was much smarter than he appeared to be.

In my subjective opinion, the bombing was not necessary to defeat the enemy.

Usually we can do without these prefaces. If we can't, we should ask what prevents us from making our claims more straightforwardly. In many cases, this sort of throat-clearing signals discomfort with our own assertions. The solution isn't to ignore or conceal that discomfort but rather to identify its source. When we see this sort of hedging in our early drafts, we should use the occasion to review what we're trying to say.

Certain verbs often flag a similar discomfort or imprecision. For example, most of us have employed *may* in the following way:

Jean Renoir *may* be the greatest director of all time.

When attached to a significant claim, this sort of hedging attracts the wrong kind of attention. It says to the audience, "Jean Renoir is the greatest director of all time—maybe. I'm not really sure, or I don't really know what I mean by that, but in any case I don't want to think the matter through to a conclusion." When used this way, verbs like *may*, *can*, and *seem* signal uncertainty, nervousness, or laziness on the author's part. In such cases, a more modest but unhedged assertion is usually more convincing than a grand claim hobbled by qualification.

Again, this sort of revision often goes beyond fixing the surface features of our sentences. In some cases, it requires us to overhaul the claim itself. Eventually we may decide to settle for something less magnificent but more precise: for example, that Renoir is a master of realism, that his visual style is first-rate, or that no director's films are more artfully structured. If supportable, any of these claims is preferable to an unstable mixture of grandiosity and tentativeness. We don't need to banish the verbs *may*, *can*, and *seem* from our papers. Rather, we need to make sure we're not misusing them to conceal a faulty claim.

O*verstating the Claim*

If hobbling our major claims is one sort of problem, another is stating them too assertively. We can avoid this problem as well by figuring out what can be said legitimately and then going on from there. Occasionally we find our own claims so compelling that we overdo the argumentation and actually invite skepticism from our readers. We signal these moments, more or less subconsciously, by overusing words like *obviously* and *clearly*, as in the following examples:

> The cover-up by the Warren Commission *clearly* indicates a conspiracy at the very highest levels.

> Homer's poems show that he *obviously* hated women.

Even if readers agree with our claims, they may not conclude that those who don't are denying the obvious. Also, experienced readers know that inexperienced writers employ this strategy exactly when things aren't clear or obvious. By using such modifiers imprecisely, we often lose credibility with these readers and make their cooperation less likely.

Notice how the following sentence creates room for skepticism:

> The fact that most Americans seem to agree with me is clear from the latest election results.

Here again we have the unstable mixture of boldness and uncertainty. What's offered up as a fact is exactly what needs to be proven: namely, that most Americans seem to agree with the author. Also, *seem* and *clear* make an unhappy couple; if things are clear, why doesn't the writer simply assert that Americans actually do agree with him?

If you spot this sort of sentence in an early draft, you should ask yourself a few questions. Is it true that most Americans agree with you? What is your evidence? How reliable is it? For example, if you're using election results as an indicator, do you need to acknowledge that most Americans don't vote? Depending on your answers to these questions, you might settle on the following: "The election results suggest that most Americans agree with me." This version is clearer, briefer, and more precise.

Such questions are inconvenient because they force us to think more critically about our own claims. Even so, there are two excellent reasons to pose them. First, they require us to anticipate audience response. By placing ourselves in the position of our readers, we are more likely to gain their cooperation. Second, the precision these questions yield makes our prose more effective. When we know more precisely what we're trying to say, we improve our chances of saying it well.

Exercise 5.2

Eliminate unnecessary modifiers and hedges, and revise for precision.

1. In my opinion, the protagonist is a very interesting character.
2. It seems to me that there are a rather large number of very obvious and significant parallels between this case and the previous one.
3. Regardless of what the polls say, the majority of Americans believe the boy should not be turned over to his father. There are sound reasons to base this judgment, but the fact that his mother risked her and her son's life for freedom in America speaks volumes. I believe it is clear that the father does not want his son so much as a foreign tyrant wants to claim a possession.
4. The local population seems to regard blood-feud as tremendously important. Chronic low-level violence clearly does not seem wholly out of place to some of them. The fact that our informant approved of vendetta seems obvious as well. I will limit my discussion to what appears to be the single most relevant episode mentioned by him during our interviews.

S *mothering the Claim*

Another problem with hedging is that it often smothers the main point, especially when it's accompanied by excessive modification. Consider the following example, culled from a book review in a prestigious periodical:

> Kissinger is inclined to believe, for example, as Winston Churchill did at the time, that Josef Stalin, when he began to realize the economic potential and staying power of the West, may have been prepared to explore the outlines of a general settlement and that the Soviet Peace Note of March 1952, raising the possibility of uniting Germany on the basis of neutrality, may have been a first step in that direction.

Did you catch that? If not, your confusion may be due to the many hedges and modifiers in this 72-word skullbuster. Let's get a better sense of this sentence's scaffolding by isolating the verbs, omitting the modifiers, and abbreviating the complements:

> Kissinger *is inclined to believe* that Josef Stalin *may have been* X, and that the Soviet Peace Note of March 1952 *may have been* Y.

Now we can see how tentative the verbs are. The author doesn't claim that Kissinger believes X and Y; rather, he tells us that Kissinger is inclined to believe that X and Y may have been the case. Even if the hedging is warranted in this instance, the obscurity of the sentence certainly isn't. Notice that the confusion isn't produced by any conceptual complexity but rather by a combination of hedged verbs and heavy modification.

If we eliminate this sentence's hedges and modifiers, we find that the underlying claim is fairly straightforward:

> Kissinger believes that Stalin was prepared to explore a general settlement, and that the Soviet Peace Note of March 1952 was a first step in that direction.

Although this version omits a good deal of information, it sacrifices very little precision. This is largely because the verb *believes* puts the rest of the sentence in the realm of speculation rather than certainty.

The author of this sentence might defend himself by noting that the revised sentence misrepresents both Kissinger's and his position. He declines to say that Kissinger believed anything, only that Kissinger was inclined to believe that something may have been the case. This sort of hedging, if taken too far, undermines the cooperative principle and most of our conversational guidelines. If I asked you whether there were any cookies left in the lunchroom, I wouldn't be satisfied to hear that you were inclined to believe that they may have been eaten; and I would be especially annoyed if it took you 72 words to communicate this minimally helpful response.

Hedging is frequently justified and even necessary, but we need to make sure our qualifications follow (rather than undermine) the guidelines of relevance, proportion, and clarity. We gain nothing, and sacrifice a good deal, if our hedging masks faulty, vague, or half-baked claims. Alert readers will see through these attempts at concealment, and even casual readers may be distracted or put off by the vagueness and obscurity.

Exercise 5.3

Revise the following passages for precision, economy, and clarity.

1. In "Man Seeking Woman," it almost seems that the author asked women what they wanted and wrote it in this ad. He comes off as a little insecure with who he is as a person.

2. I am very interested in the ESL position at Wilson High School. I strongly believe that my coursework has prepared me extremely well for the ESL position at Wilson High.

3. There is a widely spread debate in this country over the legalization of marijuana. Some people believe that its effects are highly detrimental and that it should remain illegal due to the fact that it causes insanity.

4. I believe that it is obviously in society's best interest for us to legalize drugs. Although legalization may present certain risks to society, these risks are almost certainly worth taking. It is the strong suspicion of almost all law enforcement officials that their efforts cannot do all that much to reduce drug abuse in the United States. This is clearly true of international drug enforcement efforts as well.

5. The Trojan war appears to be revenge for Helen's abduction. However, it seems as though the poem concentrates far too much on plunder for revenge to be the only motive. It seems clear that Homer's account was probably shaped more by the demands of narrative than by the actual events leading up to the siege of Troy.

6. Our research suggests that eligible families are likely to obtain adequate health care under this program and that expanding it may lead to greater family well-being. The data also indicate that urban counties have a tendency to have a somewhat higher proportion of short-term enrollees.

6

Making Connections

S*peaking Versus Writing*

Although conversation and written communication share many features, they also differ significantly. One big difference is that hearers, unlike readers, can rely on turn-taking to clear up misunderstandings. If a speaker is unclear in conversation, the hearer can always interrupt and ask for clarification. If a writer is unclear, however, readers have no such option; they can only hope that the writer has anticipated their questions and answered them elsewhere. We might view the college essay as an extended turn in a conversation, and many authors try to create a conversational feel in their writing, but written communication as such rarely permits immediate exchanges between writers and their audiences. After the writer produces the text, the audience reads it later, somewhere else, and without the writer on hand to clarify it.

Given the dynamics of written communication, the burden of clarity rests squarely on the writer. One way to bear that burden gracefully is to make clear and explicit connections between sentences and paragraphs. Forging these links can be difficult at times, but the benefits are significant. For one thing, clear connections help our readers cooperate with us. When we lead readers through our papers, we make it easier for them to recognize and appreciate our main points. When the audience has to guess at the relationship between one sentence or paragraph and the next, cooperation becomes more difficult and less likely. Making such connections isn't simply a matter of accommodating readers, however; linking our sentences and paragraphs also helps us stick to the point.

T *he Anti-Paragraph*

One way to make these connections is to make sure each paragraph focuses on and develops a single topic. Consider the opening paragraph of a student paper:

> *The Adventures of Huckleberry Finn* is a unique novel. It involves many different aspects of human existence. The story has been seen as one containing racist tendencies due to its use of racial epithets. We can't overlook that things have changed, but in the same fashion we can't change a great work of art just because it might offend someone who reads it. Now I will begin to discuss the meaning of the river and the friendship between Huck and Jim. We are very aware of the controversy this story has caused, but most of us don't know that it is also a humorous novel. This story brings up many different feelings and emotions that some readers today would find offensive.

This is a kind of anti-paragraph. Each sentence stands isolated from its neighbors, and several topics—the controversies surrounding the novel, its humor, its uniqueness, the meaning of the river, and the friendship between Huck and Jim—compete for the reader's attention. The main topic of this particular paper turned out to be the meaning of the river; but even the most cooperative audience would not apprehend this after slogging through the opening paragraph.

The second paragraph of this same draft clarifies the topic, but its sentences are also unconnected:

> The river is the connecting point from the beginning of the story to the end. The river is a main character that makes the setting very unique. Twain uses the river to show us how life can flow in many different directions. The river helps us understand how an individual's life can change within a matter of days. The river becomes a place of refuge for Huck and Jim by helping them escape danger.

Now we have the opposite problem: the topic couldn't be clearer, but the comments don't cohere. Four out of five sentences begin with the same subject ("the river"), but no sentence develops the potential of any previous one. As a result, the paragraph fails to produce a sense of progress or development.

Both of these paragraphs demonstrate the importance of making connections between sentences. They also show that successful writing balances the demands of focus and development. The first paragraph lacks focus, a conservative force that links a topic to what precedes it. The second paragraph lacks development, an innovative force that moves the discussion from point A to point B. Focus helps our readers keep the topic in mind, and development keeps them interested. What's needed in this paper, as in conversation and college writing generally, is a discussion that makes continuous progress without leaving anyone behind.

New and Given Information

In conversation, we make this sort of continuous progress by blending what linguists call new and given information. As new information is introduced into the conversation, it is commented upon and eventually becomes given or old information. New information creates a sense of direction and purpose, while given information ensures continuity and provides a backdrop against which new information can be assessed. Without new information, our writing quickly becomes repetitive and boring; without given information, it quickly becomes incomprehensible.

Needless to say, boredom and bewilderment don't set the stage for successful cooperation between you and your audience. To avoid these effects in our papers, we need to make sure the sentences and paragraphs measure and blend both types of information. This sounds complicated, but we do it more or less automatically in conversation. Once again, the challenge is to adapt our conversational habits to the different demands of written communication.

One way to make steady progress in our writing is to convert the new information of one sentence into the given information of subsequent sentences. Notice how the following paragraph, taken from a discussion of prose styles, performs this conversion:

> Plain style is communal, its model scene a congregation in which speakers reaffirm for each other common truths that are the property of all. In the theology behind plain style, truth is always simple, and it is a common human possession. Individual revisions of this communal possession distort and dilute it. The wisdom of children can be the wisdom of adults, because knowing truth requires no special experience and no critical analysis. Sophisticated thought and conceptual refinement pervert truth. Any language that reaches beyond the simplest level is suspicious as the probable symptom of such a perversion. Simple language may not always be completely adequate to the expression of truth, but at least it is pure as far as it goes. (Francis-Noël Thomas & Mark Turner, *Clear and Simple as the Truth*, 76–77)

This paragraph does several things well. First, it keeps its topic—the assumptions underlying plain style—in sharp focus. Second, each sentence contributes something new to our understanding of that topic by developing an idea or image from a preceding sentence. The image of the congregation, for example, leads to the next sentence's reference to theology.

The authors also build cohesion by reinforcing key words. In the first sentence, they assert that plain style is communal. This information is recycled in later sentences, where the authors go on to make new (but related) claims about "*common* truths," "a *common* human possession," and "revisions of this *communal* possession." By returning to key words and thereby constructing a backdrop of given information, the authors help us construe their new claims, which eventually take their own place in that backdrop.

Now watch how these authors use their description of plain style to distinguish it from what they call classic style:

> Classic style views itself as repairing the deficiency of plain style by introducing sophistication and individual responsibility. First, classic writers and readers are an elite community, consisting of those who practice the critical discipline of its theology. Anyone can take up this practice and so join, but the style is aristocratic, not egalitarian. Second, classic wisdom cannot be the wisdom of children because it depends upon a wealth of adult experience. In plain style, everyone is equal; truth is everyone's birthright. It is seen by all; it is everyone's possession. It can come out of the mouths of babes. In classic style, truth is available to all who are willing to work to achieve it, but truth is certainly not commonly possessed by all and is no one's birthright. In the classic view, truth is the possession of individuals who have validated common wisdom; for them, truth has been achieved, and such achievement requires both experience and a critical intelligence beyond the range of babes.

Here again the authors cultivate one idea carefully and intensively. Notice that the emphasis on commonality is continued by way of the many references to community, what is and is not commonly possessed, and the status of common wisdom. The authors develop this idea further by adding a new claim: that classic style, unlike plain style, requires us to validate common wisdom with adult experience and critical analysis. Because it proceeds from a solid foundation of given information, this line of thinking creates a sense of controlled progress. Once again, the authors reinforce key terms, sometimes with slight variation, to make their points. For example, the repetition of the word *practice* links the second and third sentences, while the two clauses in the last sentence are joined by the alternation of *achieved* and *achievement*.

This skillful blending of new and given information creates cohesion, clarity, and a sense of purpose, all of which characterize a cogent practical style. Of course, we may not always want to be cogent. At times we may wish to mystify, bore, or pacify our audience. In such cases, incoherence and obscurity can be very effective. But this strategy rarely works with college readers, who usually want to understand things better. In fact, these readers may not agree with our conclusions even when our prose is clear and cohesive. By delivering them from unnecessary guesswork and puzzlement, however, we put such disagreements on a different and more productive footing.

N ominalization

In Chapter 2, we converted nouns into verbs to animate our sentences. Instead of writing "The new technology caused a *transformation* of society," we preferred "The new technology *transformed* society." Sometimes, however, we need to reverse that process and convert verbs and other parts of speech into nouns. This conversion, called *nominalization*, works especially well when we want to recycle the new information of a previous sentence. Notice how nominalization builds connections between the following pairs of sentences:

> The new technology *transformed* society. Although it was felt most keenly in the cities, this *transformation* affected the rural population as well.

> Sometimes we *convert* verbs into nouns. Whatever else they may do, such *conversions* build cohesion.

> The campaign to refurbish the harbor was extraordinarily *successful*. Most city planners attribute this *success* to several factors.

> Sophisticated thought and conceptual refinement *pervert* truth. Any language that reaches beyond the simplest level is suspicious as the probable symptom of such a *perversion*.

Nominalization of this sort builds explicit links between sentences. The links needn't be this obvious to achieve cohesion, however. We may prefer synonyms, for example, especially when the nominalizations sound too repetitive or predictable. In general, however, it's easier to soften the links between sentences than it is to forge them in the first place. If a paragraph lacks shape and direction, converting the verb (or adjective) of one sentence into a noun in the subsequent one often helps get the paragraph back on track.

Exercise 6.1

Nominalize the verb of the first sentence to fit the second sentence.

1. In June, management decided that the entire line needed a new advertising campaign. This _____ was supported by the July sales figures.

2. The new immigrants prospered for the next several decades. Their _____ has been attributed to a number of factors.

3. The politicians thought they perceived a shift in the public's attitudes. Still, there were many signs that this _____ was inaccurate.

4. Trade and production continued to deteriorate as a result of these policies. The empire was locked in a vicious circle in which responses to this _____ diminished the chances of recovery.

5. This most recent book, for example, omits any mention of research conducted in the last fifteen years. The _____ is all the more unusual given the author's stated goal of evaluating the effects of this research on current practice.

A ntecedents

So far we have emphasized the importance of cohesion in our writing. Now it's time to consider a common threat to that cohesion: the unclear antecedent. The term *antecedent* (Latin for "what goes before") refers to the noun or noun-equivalent for which a pronoun stands. In the following sentences, the underlined pronouns refer to the capitalized antecedents:

HADLEY doesn't know it, but <u>she</u> is getting a puppy for <u>her</u> birthday.

Although THE PUPPY is a beagle, <u>it</u> looks like a chicken.

IT'S THE RUNT OF THE LITTER, but I don't think <u>that</u> will matter much.

When a pronoun or demonstrative (*he, she, it, this*) doesn't obviously refer to what precedes it, we say that the antecedent is unclear. These loose connections between pronouns and their antecedents weaken cohesion in our writing. Consider the following passage:

> About 60 percent of college graduates never read a book after receiving their degrees. About 30 percent never read a book written by someone other than Stephen King. This shows that Americans are reading less now than ever before.

Notice that the grammatical subject of the last sentence isn't especially clear. When an author writes, "*This* shows that x, y, and z," we sometimes want to ask, "This *what*, exactly?" In our example we can hazard a guess; *this* probably refers to the statistics cited in the previous sentences. But loose connections can produce more complex interpretive problems, as in the following (my emphasis):

> Prufrock has taken the time to notice her light brown hair and the scent of her perfume, but should he presume that she would want to be with him when he is balding and aging and confused? Despite all of his tears and prayers, *it* is really nothing in the end. Despite his strength, he has seen death.

Here the word *it* could refer to tears and prayers, but the previous sentence suggests that the antecedent may be self-doubt, confusion, or some other anguish. We don't really know what the author has in mind. Worse yet, she may not know either.

At first blush, unclear antecedents seem to be local problems only fussy English teachers would bother to notice or mention. However, these local problems often conceal more general ones. To clarify the antecedent in the previous example, we would have to think more precisely about the claim itself. What is it, precisely, that "is really nothing in the end"? If we can answer that question, we're in a much better position to proceed with our argument. If we can't answer it, we need to ask why not and consider appropriate changes. Again, this example shows that careful revision doesn't decorate a preexisting meaning; rather, it helps to create and shape a precise meaning.

Exercise 6.2

Identify the unclear antecedents.

1. As a society, we look upon the upper class as having the good life. We might also view them as lucky. Those might not always be true, but some people strive to find that lifestyle.

2. Obviously it is not bad for these fathers to have their dreams, but it must also coordinate with the child's dreams as well.

3. For a long time, the mob profited from casinos and other operations in Cuba. Once Castro came to power, they stood a good chance of losing a billion-dollar business.

4. In the memo, the chief financial officer told his assistant that he would run the next audit. This was not considered unusual at the time.

5. The Mediterranean basin stressed a group ethic based on kinship and gender rather than individualism based on economics and property. Its pivotal moral values were rooted in honor and shame as well as patronage and clientage. This was challenged by the practice of open commensality, or communal eating without regard for social distinction.

Transitions

When conversing, we constantly signal relationships between our contributions and the conversation as a whole. We do that signaling with what linguists call *discourse markers*. Discourse markers are words and phrases that mean little or nothing by themselves but which indicate how our utterances are meant to fit the conversation. Here are some examples:

> *Well*, I wouldn't say that.
>
> And I was, *like*, no way!
>
> I *just* wanted to see if you were free this evening.
>
> I was starting to lose my patience, *y'know*?

These discourse markers perform a range of subtle but important duties. For example, the phrase *y'know* is often used in conversation to present new information as if it were given information. Most of these discourse markers are too informal for college writing, and they rarely show up in our essays and reports. Even so, the sort of work they do is even more important in writing than in conversation, mostly because writers must be more explicit than speakers when it comes to signaling relationships between sentences and the discourse as a whole. Accordingly, we can and should learn other ways to signal these relationships in our writing.

One way to connect sentences is with *transitional phrases*, which indicate the relationship between two or more sentences. Below are some typical relationships, along with the transitional phrases that signal them:

RELATION	TRANSITIONAL PHRASES
Addition	and, also, furthermore, in addition, moreover, besides, too, finally
Contrast	but, however, nevertheless, although, on the other hand, instead, rather
Comparison	likewise, similarly, in the same way
Exemplification	for example, for instance, in particular
Logical	so, therefore, then, consequently, thus, as a result, accordingly, if . . . then
Temporal	after, next, since, while, during, meanwhile, before, at the same time

Experienced readers are on the lookout for such transitional phrases because they mark out an interpretive path through a paper. Clear transitions help the reader cooperate with you, but clumsy marking, or none at all, forces the reader to guess at the relationship between one sentence and the next.

Notice how transitional phrases are used in the following passage, which discusses the role of literary theory in American universities:

> Even now, *however*, I feel that some methodological caution is required. *To be sure*, class and status decidedly play a role in the incidence of belief in this or that literary theory. *Yet* the connections, as I will try to indicate, are often ironic rather than straightforward. *Furthermore*, it is impossible to infer from the known class and status of a literary theorist what the content of his theory is likely to be. It would take a very keen sociologist, *for example*, to detect major differences of class and status between literary professors at Harvard and those at Yale. *Yet* from the standpoint of literary theory, a brief trip between Cambridge and New Haven would be like a journey to the moon. (Frederick Crews, *Skeptical Engagements*, 115–16)

As an exercise, try reading this paragraph without the italicized phrases. You'll find that it's more difficult to follow, mostly because we have to construct the connections provided in the original version. Once again, these connections help writers as well as readers; when we make the relationships between our sentences explicit, it's easier to control the shape and direction of our papers.

At the beginning of this chapter I claimed that authors bear the burden of clarity. I also suggested that making clear connections is one way to bear that burden gracefully. This conception of writing sounds strenuous, as well it should; revision can be hard work. But our exertions are most effective when they appear effortless. For this reason, it's best to construct and polish these connections at the draft stage: offstage, as it were, so that the transitions in the final paper look easy, fluid, and inevitable. Jean Renoir, who may be the best film director of all time, once observed that the best editing is the kind that isn't noticed. So it is with revision. As you edit your papers to eliminate gaps, jumps, and cuts that might distract your audience, remember that your hard work makes your reader's cooperation easier, likelier, and more productive.

Exercise 6.3

Revise the following passages, paying special attention to connections between sentences.

1. Action movies are very popular now. I don't like them. These movies are more interested in explosions and car chases than in character and plot. In *Cliffhanger*, the director seems to put all his creative energy into the opening sequence.

2. The linguist was struck by the man's speech patterns. They were characteristic of the local dialect. She had little interest in him as a person. When he asked her to be his teacher, her curiosity was aroused.

3. There have been many critics who have written about this poem. Most of the critics agree that religion is a major theme throughout the work of art. I think that religion clearly is important, but I would argue that other themes are even more central.

7

Mixing It Up

R *hythm, Sound, and Emphasis*

Economy is an important feature of practical style, but the shortest sentence doesn't always win the prize. The reason for this becomes clear when we begin to arrange sentences into paragraphs. A string of short, choppy sentences often comes off worse than a sequence of longer ones of varying length and structure. We shouldn't conclude from this observation, however, that the shorter sentences need to be padded with meaningless verbiage. Rather, the key is to combine sentences to create new ones that vary in length, rhythm, sound, and emphasis. These last qualities play an important role in generating reader interest, aiding comprehension, and creating memorable sentences and paragraphs. Even as we revise our sentences for economy, then, we should look for effective ways to vary and arrange them.

Perhaps the easiest way to begin thinking about sentence variety is to read our prose aloud and with emphasis. As we do, we shouldn't expect our writing to sound conversational; after all, very few of us speak in complete sentences and polished paragraphs. The exercise is useful, however, because it allows us to hear stylistic and grammatical problems that are often difficult to see. For example, the passage from the Huck Finn paper sounds especially flat and monotonous when read aloud:

> The river is the connecting point from the beginning of the story to the end. The river itself is a main character which makes the setting unique. Twain uses the river to show us how life can flow in many different directions. The river helps us understand how an individual's life can change within a matter of days. The river becomes a place of refuge for Huck and Jim by helping them escape danger.

The first thing we hear in this passage is an all-too-predictable emphasis on one phrase, "the river." In this case, the echo doesn't add power or cohesion, as controlled repetition sometimes does. Whether or not we see the repetition, we will almost certainly hear it. After years of listening to conversation, radio, and television, our ears detect the false notes and dull refrains that frequently escape our eyes.

One thing we won't hear in the Huck Finn paragraph is a variety of sentence lengths and structures. Two of these sentences have 15 words apiece, two have 16 words, and one has 12 words. It's difficult to create a dynamic effect when sentence lengths are so similar. Also, each sentence proceeds in a subject-verb-object pattern without any attempt at transition from one sentence to the next. Even if we prefer this sentence pattern in most situations, we need to make smooth transitions and vary the pattern from time to time. Again, we may not see that our sentences are becoming predictable, but we will hear it. We needn't count words or diagram sentences to make sure that our sentences are sufficiently varied in length and structure; simply reading them aloud alerts us to problems in this area.

Let's try another passage from a student draft:

> At the beginning of the novel, the narrator believes that all things are clear to him; however, he comes to realize that he cannot understand himself as he changes. He has no insight into the person that he has become. The only thing that is clear to him by the end of the novel is that nothing is clear. The only thing that he gets is his own image staring back at him. He cannot see anyone and he cannot understand anyone; his own vanity makes that impossible.

After reading this passage aloud, the author decided that her last three sentences sounded flat. Because they contained her major claim, she wanted to get them right. Revising for economy and variety, she arrived at the following:

> Initially the narrator believes that all things are clear to him. He comes to realize, however, that he does not understand the person he has become. By the end of the novel, the only thing he can discern is his own image staring back at him. He cannot truly see or understand anyone, including himself, because his own vanity precludes that possibility.

The second version is briefer and clearer than the original, but another advantage is that it sounds better. For starters, it cuts down on the repetition; instead of consecutive sentences with the same opening ("The only thing that . . . "), she has kept one such sentence.

Likewise, "He cannot see anyone and he cannot understand anyone" becomes "He cannot truly see or understand anyone." Shortening this sentence allows her to combine it with the subsequent one; that change, in turn, varies the sentence lengths and rhythms and emphasizes the logical link between the last two clauses. In this case, that link is especially important because it introduces a major claim. Finally, by repeating an initial consonant ("precludes that possibility"), she creates a more memorable clinching sentence. This shorter, clearer, and more rhythmical first paragraph gets this essay off to a better start.

Here's another sample from a student draft:

> Higgins did his best to conceal any attraction to Eliza. He worked with Eliza for six months teaching her to speak correctly. During this time Higgins grew more and more fond of her. Higgins and Pickering continued to groom Eliza. Her ability to speak was tested at Higgins's mother's home and at social events.

When read aloud, this passage doesn't flow very well. For one thing, the name Higgins is repeated too frequently. When we hear this sort of repetition, we should start looking for ways to combine sentences in order to minimize it. For example, the first sentence can be combined with the third one, which makes a similar point. Such combinations help vary the sentence patterns as well. Finally, the passage lacks transitional modifiers that would help smooth the way. With a few minor adjustments, the revised paragraph reads as follows:

> For six months, Higgins taught Eliza to speak correctly. Although he grew more and more fond of her, he did his best to conceal his feelings. Both he and Pickering continued to train and groom Eliza, whose ability to speak was tested at Higgins's mother's home and at social events.

The content of this passage is largely unchanged, but the new paragraph makes smoother transitions and varies sentence lengths and structures.

Exercise 7.1

Read the following passages aloud, and revise for sound, variety, rhythm, and emphasis.

1. Today's welfare system is shaped by years of federal legislation. It involves a close partnership between the federal and state govern-

ments. The federal government dictates the major features of the state programs.

2. *Sir Gawain and the Green Knight* offers the reader a lesson in proper decorum and courtly manners. The author of this work uses knighthood as an example of decency and goodness. The moral and social values offered to the reader in *Sir Gawain and the Green Knight* are portrayed in the actions of Sir Gawain.

3. We must develop new procedures with which to document and validate writing assessment. While traditional writing assessment procedures rely on statistical validation and standardization, new writing assessment methods will need to employ more qualitative validation procedures. The validation methods summarized above can serve as models for documenting new writing assessment procedures.

4. Although it seems that Willa Cather's *Death Comes for the Archbishop* is a story about the lifelong relationship between Father Latour and Father Joseph, I think it is a book of contrasts. The book contrasts different cultures, times, and personalities. Cather contrasts the cultures of the indigenous peoples of America with the European cultures. It also contrasts the past, present, and future. Also, Cather contrasts the personalities of Father Latour and Father Joseph.

5. In 1921, Keynes completed a book titled *A Treatise on Probability.* He began work on it after graduating from Cambridge. He worked on it for approximately 15 years after graduation. He struggled to convey new ideas with clarity. He never quite broke away from his training in philosophy at Cambridge, which placed a great emphasis on clarity.

S *trong Endings*

When the first part of a sentence is in order, readers find themselves on solid ground. The topic is clear, the characters are properly staged, and the action is specified. The last part of a sentence, however, frequently moves the reader toward less familiar and more complex ideas. Experienced readers expect this pattern and therefore like the last part of the sentence to be especially clear and emphatic. If we wish to satisfy that expectation, our endings need to be as carefully considered as our verbs and agents. Again, our readers aren't the only ones who benefit from this clarity; when we finish a sentence well, it's easier to make a smooth transition to the next sentence and thereby create a clear sense of direction.

One way to end sentences well is to make sure the final words and phrases don't trail off or divert us from the main point. These effects occur when a sentence ends with unimportant, unnecessary, or irrelevant information. Here's an example of a sentence that needs trimming at the end:

> F. Scott Fitzgerald's *The Great Gatsby* critiques the pretenses set up by the characters involved in the story.

Revising for economy, we get the following:

> F. Scott Fitzgerald's *The Great Gatsby* critiques the pretenses of its characters.

Notice that everything in the original after the word "characters" vanishes. Good riddance: The phrase "involved in the story" is anticlimactic and ends the sentence on a weak note.

Here's a longer passage that needs the same sort of revision:

> The minister is an unusual character whom we cannot easily identify with, as are most of the characters in the novel. He is not idealized, and expresses that he even feels very enslaved to himself. His brutal honesty with himself often reveals self-truths that abruptly confront the reader. Although in the long run his actions are unproductive, they reveal the virtue within the character of the minister.

No flow, weak endings, a few redundancies, and questionable diction, but also a lot of potential: in short, the sort of passage that repays our efforts at revision. Let's see what the author did with the first sentence:

> The minister, like most of the characters in the novel, is an unusual character with whom we cannot easily identify.

This version puts the important new information where it belongs: at the end of the sentence. It's not the minister's similarity to other characters that's important, but rather his character and our reaction to it. Notice that this version doesn't end the first clause with the preposition *with*. Some sticklers say we should never end a clause with a preposition; but even if that "rule" seems too strict, we still have the problem that a preposition is difficult to stress. Accordingly, many writers prefer to end their sentences with key nouns or verbs.

Next, the author decided to delete the last part of the second sentence, and combine what was left with the original third sentence:

He is not idealized, and his brutal self-honesty often reveals truths that abruptly confront the reader.

And then:

Although the minister's actions are futile, they reveal his inner virtue.

Putting it all together:

The minister, like most of the characters in the novel, is an unusual character with whom we cannot easily identify. He is not idealized, and his brutal self-honesty often reveals truths that abruptly confront the reader. Although finally the minister's actions are futile, they reveal his inner virtue.

Try reading both paragraphs aloud and with emphasis. You'll find that in the revised version, the stress tends to fall where it does the most good, namely, toward the end of the sentences.

In this chapter, we've addressed what might be called the aesthetics of practical style. Although this style rarely calls attention to its own charms, it works best when it harnesses the natural cadences of the English language. The aesthetic dimension of practical style can't be ignored if we want our writing to achieve its aims. By reading aloud and revising for sound, rhythm, and emphasis, we make our prose more graceful and effective. William Morris, the nineteenth-century designer and author, once said that we should have nothing in our homes that we do not know to be useful or believe to be beautiful. We might say the same about our writing, adding that utility and beauty are not mutually exclusive.

Exercise 7.2

Revise for economy, paying special attention to endings.

1. The transformation comes through a series of experiences and journeys that make him a fully reasoning, understanding, and thoughtful man in adulthood.

2. Many people simply watch the events of life as they unfold rather than taking a role in how they are played out.

3. These persons are preoccupied with oddities relative to society.

4. In Willa Cather's *Death Comes for the Archbishop*, there are very strongly bonded relationships. The strongest is the relationship between the two main characters, Father Latour and Father Vaillant. Father Vaillant is the first to die and he leaves Father Latour lonely, and left only with his memories of their shared experiences and lifetimes. In a sunken state of a broken heart, Father Latour dies of

caused by the

loneliness and a void in his being and heart left by the death of his best friend and companion, Father Vaillant.

5. Greece was a collection of loosely connected city-states known as the Mycenaean League. The league was organized in such a way that the whole conglomeration of city-states could work together to accomplish a single objective, such as the destruction of Troy on one extreme, or all of them could act independently of one another on the opposite extreme.

8

Saying What You Mean

S *ome Useful Routines*

So far we have emphasized revision and its benefits. By now the reason for this emphasis should be clear. Although we don't always have something worthy to say when we start writing a paper, we often develop something suitable or even important to say by the time our deadline rolls around. Some writers, however, prefer a different strategy. Faced with a Friday morning deadline, they stay up late Thursday night and crank out a last-minute, caffeine-addled rapture. If executed properly, this method allows its practitioners to believe that revision is an unaffordable luxury. Of course, some writing must be done quickly and under the gun, but the last-minute approach is often a way of avoiding the more strenuous (if less dramatic) alternative of starting early, revising often, and ruthlessly eliminating all that is irrelevant and obscure.

Unfortunately, even ruthless elimination doesn't guarantee good writing. Revision is crucial, but it does nothing to diminish the dual horrors of the blank page and the deadline. To revise well, we must do more than trim what doesn't belong in our papers; we must also identify and build on the most promising parts of our early drafts. Again, there are no rules for deciding which sentences and paragraphs have potential or how to tap it most effectively. Even so, we can develop useful routines for cultivating our ideas-in-progress. In this chapter, we will focus on identifying our best formulations, developing them carefully, and using them to generate larger units of writing.

S *lowing Down*

One common problem, especially at the draft stage, is trying to say too much in a single paragraph. Instead of developing one idea, we telegraph several and hope for the best. This practice makes audience cooperation difficult. Even if our readers want to, they can't follow our line of thinking. Another problem with an overloaded paragraph is that we often lose our own sense of direction. We've seen several examples of this already, including the opening paragraph of the Huck Finn paper:

> *The Adventures of Huckleberry Finn* by Mark Twain is a unique novel. It involves many aspects of human existence. The story is always under great criticism by publishers of many races and nationalities. This story has been seen as one containing racist tendencies. We can't overlook that things have changed, but in the same fashion we can't change a great work of art just because it might offend someone who reads it. Now I will begin to discuss the meaning of the river and the friendship between Huck and Jim. It is common knowledge that we are very unaware of the controversy this story has with the public, but most of us don't know that it also was depicted as a humorous novel. This story brings up many different feelings and emotions which some readers today would find offensive.

This paragraph has too many balls in the air at the same time. It introduces a provocative topic, racism, only to dismiss it and take up two other topics: the meaning of the river and Huck and Jim's friendship. Before developing either of these, however, it lurches back to the controversy surrounding the novel's reception. Given that the next paragraph focuses on the river, the author would do well to use the first paragraph to introduce that topic. There's no single way to do this, but some ways are better than others. Many authors would begin by stressing the importance of the river to the novel as a whole, or by noting the amount of critical attention the topic has received over the years. However we arrive at our main topic, though, we shouldn't rush through it once it has been introduced. Instead, we're better off proceeding slowly, making sure that each important point receives adequate attention.

There are at least two good reasons to slow down around our major points. First, we're more likely to make those points effectively if we assume that our readers don't already know what we're thinking. When we've been pondering something for a while, we frequently assume that our readers have been doing the same. This mistake prompts us to race through the very points that must be developed thoroughly if our papers are to succeed. Second, we don't always discover what it is we want to say until we begin to explore the language of our early drafts. These discoveries frequently lead us to abandon whole sections of our drafts, but they also lead us to fresh ideas and more effective ways to develop them. By unpacking our main points more methodically, we often find new things to say and better ways to say them.

By way of illustration, suppose you have settled on a topic and sketched out some paragraphs, but you've come to a dead end. Tragically, you have only three pages of what is supposed to be a five-page assignment. Now what? One option is to keep repeating your claims until you get to five pages. Another is to widen the margins and switch to a larger font. A less convenient but more effective option is to develop and enrich what you've already written. In the following paragraph, for example, the main points are fairly distinct, but a little extra development would help:

> Arguments for a half-cent sales tax increase for economic development are defying a law of economics, which states "you don't increase the price of a product to sell more of that product." Local sales and services are this community's product. A no vote on the sales tax is a vote of compassion for low-income citizens as well as a vote of concern for our local businessmen who collect local taxes, which shouldn't be used against them to subsidize competition from the outside.

A careful reading of this paragraph turns up four separate claims. The first is that increasing the price of a product leads to less demand for that product. (This point could be followed with a more straightforward assertion, such as "When the price of a product goes up, people buy less of that product.") The second point is that higher taxes raise the price of local goods and services. According to the first claim, this price increase leads to less demand for those goods and services. The third point is that this particular kind of price increase hurts poor people more than anyone else. (This claim needs more support; the author might note that rich people buy more than poor people and therefore pay more sales tax, but that poor people pay out a higher percentage of their income on such taxes.) The fourth point is that the new tax would hurt local businesspeople, not only because their products would be more expensive than those in neighboring communities, but also because the revenues would be used to subsidize new firms moving to the community; some of these new firms, in turn, might take away customers from established businesses.

By separating and restating these four points, we create new possibilities for expanding and strengthening the argument. Such a restatement makes each point clearer and more distinct, and disentangling the claims and presenting them sequentially adds power to the overall argument against the new tax. If we want to elaborate that argument, we've certainly found a way to do it; the restatement easily doubles the length of the original passage. We could go on to support each one of these four points with facts, figures, examples, relevant comments from experts, and so on. In short, this short passage could become a five-paragraph essay—if we know how to slow down, identify the main points, and use them to generate larger units of discourse.

Developing Your Ideas

Another way to develop and enrich a draft is to rummage through earlier sentences for words, images, or ideas that can be amplified or expanded. As the previous example shows, first drafts often contain too many rather than too few possibilities, so the key is to isolate the ones with real potential. In the following passage, for example, the author has only begun to probe the key ideas:

> In this episode, the narrator is seen as going through a rite of passage. The transformation comes through the experiences of life that make him a thoughtful adult. He goes from being a spectator to understanding that it isn't enough to just observe. All of this can be seen through the changing tone of the descriptions throughout the novel.

With the help of her peer editors, the author of this paragraph saw two possibilities for developing it. The first was to focus on the notion of transformation, which would mean expanding the "rite of passage" part of the paragraph. The other was to develop the idea of spectatorship and the obligations of the observer. She also realized that these two notions could be linked more firmly within the paragraph. Finally, she felt the last sentence was vague and needed strengthening.

Here's what she came up with:

> In this episode, the narrator goes through a rite of passage that transforms him into a thoughtful adult. In particular, he goes from being a childlike spectator, albeit a keen one, to recognizing his own participation in (and responsibility for) the world he observes. As this feeling begins to take hold, his detached spectatorship gives way to greater empathy, a broader range of adult emotions, and more interest in other people. At the same time, his own language becomes more lyrical and complex. Whereas his descriptions early in the novel are

strictly visual and objective, detailing the slightest changes in light and color, the later descriptions are deeper and more reflective.

Here each sentence grows out of previous ones—notice the use of transitional phrases—and develops the connection between spectatorship and the character's transformation. Also, the gaps in the original version are filled. For example, the original paragraph notes that the character realizes "it isn't enough just to observe." This formulation raises several questions: why isn't it enough? What is enough? Enough for what? Even if the author doesn't give complete answers in this paragraph, she ought to have them clearly in mind by the time she works through the final draft. Ditto for the original last sentence, which notes the changing tone of the narrator's descriptions but gives no clue as to the nature or direction of that change. Finally, adding the word *reflective* chimes well with the author's interest in vision and spectatorship. This grace note helps bring the revised paragraph to a satisfactory conclusion.

Notice that in expanding this passage, we didn't pad it with fluff or pointless repetition. Instead, we identified the best ideas and treated them in more detail. As we learn to unpack our ideas more deliberately, however, we shouldn't forget about our desire to eliminate unnecessary language. We still want to shed verbiage, but sometimes we can only determine which parts are truly necessary after we've discovered, through a process of expansion and revision, exactly what we want to say.

Exercise 8.1

Expand the following paragraphs by identifying main points and developing them more carefully.

1. There are several good reasons to attend college today. More and more, college degrees are required for good jobs. Also, advancement often depends on abilities and attitudes acquired in college such as communication skills, reasoning ability, intellectual and emotional maturity, and general knowledge of our culture as well as familiarity with other cultures.

2. High textbook prices are bad for publishers as well as students. As prices go up, more and more students are forced to share books or sell them back at the end of the semester. Sometimes they even copy books illegally. Also, authors are not paid royalties on the sale of used books, which makes them more reluctant to write textbooks in the first place.

3. I like to read biographies because they are informative and tell me what it was like to live in a particular time. They explain why the subject was successful and how he or she got to be that way. They make history interesting.

E xploring Your Own Metaphors

Another way to elaborate ideas is to explore the most promising metaphors in our own drafts. Although metaphors are often seen as fancy literary ornaments, they're better understood as basic tools in our ordinary conceptual system. In fact, our everyday conversations are full of metaphors. For example, we think and talk about politics in terms of sports:

> The President's speech was a home run.

We think and talk about time as a precious resource:

> We wasted a lot of time on that.

And so on. Notice that we're not being especially fancy or literary when we say someone wasted our time; rather, this is the ordinary way of thinking about time in our culture.

Because metaphor is a basic tool in our conceptual system, our own metaphors frequently reveal our general approach to a given topic. When we use a metaphor, we assume or endorse a particular way of understanding that topic. For example, when we say that the President's speech was a home run, we suggest an underlying conceptual link between politics and baseball. Of course, there are other ways to understand political speeches, many of which have nothing to do with sports. For instance, we also talk about political speeches in terms of healing, navigating, building bridges, and so on. Each of these metaphors suggests something different about the nature, purpose, and effects of political speeches. The metaphor we choose, then, tells us something about which aspects of the speech and its effects we wish to highlight.

As we take more notice of the metaphors in our early drafts, we find that they suggest ways of elaborating our ideas and generating new ones. Consider this opening sentence from an essay on stylistic revision:

> Fighting clutter is like fighting weeds—the writer is always slightly behind. New varieties sprout overnight, and by noon they are part of American speech. It only takes a John Dean testifying on TV to have everyone in the country saying "at this point in time" instead of "now." (William Zinsser, "Clutter")

The governing metaphor here—that extra words are weeds—implies that these words are undesirable, that they should be removed, and that they prevent more beautiful or important language from flourishing. If we understand the metaphor, we apprehend the qualities shared by weeds and verbiage. We also ignore the qualities they don't share. For example, we don't conclude that verbiage is green, or leafy, or bad for our hay fever; instead, we make the relevant connection between weeds and verbiage, and we use what we know about the former to structure our understanding of the latter.

Suppose you had written these sentences about clutter in an early draft, but that you had bogged down shortly thereafter. Exploring your own metaphor can help you get back on track. You might begin with a series of questions about the metaphor itself. What does the weed metaphor suggest about the topic? Do those suggestions help you make your points more effectively? Why or why not? If the weed metaphor is apt, how can you build on its strengths? Which related metaphors might be useful in developing your claims? Would it be helpful, for instance, to think of essays as gardens and stylistic revision as weeding? Or would it be better to think of stylistic revision as a journey, a discovery, or as sunshine burning off fog? These questions are worth asking even if you never refer to weeds again. Because your own metaphors suggest an approach to your topic and claim, exploring them offers you an opportunity to develop and refine that approach. Having done so, you will find that your claim is that much easier to advance. Far from being fancy decorations or finishing touches, our metaphors become potential sources of new material.

In addition to generating material, good metaphors also guide readers through our papers. A well-chosen metaphor advances our points, often by suggesting more than can be said explicitly in a given context. In contrast, a poor metaphor distracts our readers or even works against our purposes by suggesting all the wrong things. Consider the following metaphor, which appeared in the first sentence of a student paper:

> Cognitive science has taken the university by storm.

This metaphor seems ill-suited to the topic. Taking something by storm sounds violent, perhaps too violent in this case; we don't usually think of a new science attacking the institution that created and nurtured it. This particular metaphor is also a cliché. Images of invasion and conquest, especially routine ones, probably won't lead to a rich new understanding of this topic.

Sometimes the metaphors we choose don't work together well. The classic case is the mixed metaphor, as in the following:

> Congratulations to the President for orchestrating this nation into uncharted waters.

Orchestrate is fine, as is *uncharted waters*, but not both. (Perhaps the easiest remedy here is to change *orchestrating* to *navigating* or *steering*.) We should note, however, that distinct metaphors aren't bound to clash. Some metaphors combine to create rich, resonant images and effects. But if we find that our metaphors aren't especially helpful in organizing, conveying, or generating ideas, we should try to figure out what isn't working. Again, this rethinking may go beyond removing the metaphors; it may involve recasting our major ideas. That effort will be repaid, however, if it leads to a clearer conception of the topic.

Exercise 8.2

Write a paragraph expanding each of the following metaphors.

1. Television is a vast cultural wasteland.
2. Television is electronic junk food.
3. Here at United Consolidated, we're one big family.
4. When students arrive at the university, they ought to be treated right. After all, they are the customers; they should get a good product for their money.
5. Universities are important national treasures. We should subsidize them for the same reason we subsidize national parks like Yellowstone or Yosemite.

Readings

Personal Ads

Man Seeking Woman

ABOUT TO QUIT TRYING—I've been looking for her for a long time. The results of my efforts are appalling. I'm almost convinced she doesn't exist. She's between 21 and 35, attractive, not over-weight, and has a good personality, a great sense of humor, and a strong sense of monogamy. Are you out there? I'm 36, medium height and build, above average intelligence and personality. I'm humorous, thoughtful, and sharp-witted. Governed by a sharp sense of self determination, sense of humor, and a variety of inter-ests and experiences, I enjoy people who are not afraid to try and can fend for themselves. I'm far from dull and always looking for new and exciting things to do. Self-absorbed people bore me. I'm compassionate, romantic, and great fun to be with. I'm attractive and can actualy carry on an intelligent conversation on a number of subjects. I'm mostly disappointed in the women I've met, per-haps because we never met.

Questions

1. Would you like to meet this person? Why or why not? Which parts of the ad make you feel the way you do?
2. Consider the writer's diction, or choice of words. How well does the word *appalling* work in the second sentence? How about the typographical error "actualy" in the penultimate sentence? Which other words help or hurt the author's chances of meeting someone?
3. What is the author's favorite topic?

4. Consider the sentence starting with "Governed by a sharp sense of self determination . . ." Does this sentence help the author? Why or why not? Is the word *governed* compatible with what follows?

5. The author tells us twice that he has a good sense of humor. Do you think he does? Why or why not?

Woman Seeking Man

I'm multi-racial (consider myself African American), 5'8", presently and temporarily above my normal weight of 135, hair auburn, eyes brown, wear corrective lenses (nearsighted), born in the year of the dragon. I am open to a forever relationship with right man who fits this profile: 6'1" to 6'5", weight in proportion to height, a youthful 40 to 60 years of age, fit, healthy and active, not from dysfunctional background, no dependents or baggage from the past, non-smoker, disease, alcohol and drug free, no annoying or disgusting habits, not bigoted, negative, or have low self-esteem, not into casual or recreational sex, a professional, businessman, or entrepreneur with many and varied interests who is comfortable in his own skin, not afraid to cry or be in touch with his feelings, well-mannered, progressive, intelligent, communicative, articulate, personable, mature, well-adjusted, high morals, values, dependable, easy-going, kind, caring, loving, sensitive, considerate, patient, healthy sex attitudes, meticulously clean, neat, and orderly, dresses appropriately for the occasion, if jewelry worn must be understated and the very best quality. A one-woman man who is romantic, who thoroughly loves and likes women, who is expert in the art of courtship, likes pets, nature, an appreciation for the finer things in life, prefers quality to quantity, always puts toilet seat down, and believes in a supreme being. All of the above is non-negotiable. A real plus if you enjoy cooking, have a moustache, slightly bowed legs, and drive a Lexus or Infiniti.

Questions

1. Would you like to meet this person? Why or why not? Which parts of the ad make you feel the way you do?

2. Read the ad aloud. Which stylistic features are accentuated?

3. How much information does the author offer about herself? Is it well measured? Relevant? How about the information regarding her "right man"?

4. What can you gather about the author from her diction? For starters, you might consider her use of the words *dysfunctional*, *self-esteem*, and *baggage*.
5. Consider the way the author ends her sentences, especially the longer ones. What effects are created by these endings? Do you think they are intentional? Why or why not?

*Francis-Noël Thomas
& Mark Turner*

Francis-Noël Thomas is Professor of Humanities at Truman College in Chicago. His other work includes *The Writer Writing: Philosophic Acts in Literature*. Mark Turner is Professor of English at the University of Maryland and the author or co-author of many books on the cognitive dimensions of literature, art, and the social sciences, including *The Literary Mind, Death is the Mother of Beauty,* and *More Than Cool Reason: A Field Guide to Poetic Metaphor.*

from *Clear and Simple as the Truth: Writing Classic Prose*

1   *I*n the model scene behind practical style, the reader has a problem to solve, a decision to make, a ruling to hand down, an inquiry to conduct, a machine to design or repair—in short, a job to do. The reader's need, not the writer's desire to articulate something, initiates the writing. The writer's job is to serve the reader's immediate need by delivering timely materials. The motive can thus be almost anything productive of a need: greed, enterprise, competition, philanthropy. Since the reader is engaged in solving a problem, the reading is not an end in itself, it is instrumental to some other end. That is why, in this scene, the prime literary virtue is ease of parsing. In practical style, the best presentation will allow the reader to acquire timely information with a minimum of distraction because, in this scene, writing is an instrument for delivering information with maximum efficiency and in such a way as to place the smallest possible burden upon the reader, who has other—more important—burdens to bear.

2   In classic style, by contrast, neither writer nor reader has a job, the writing and reading do not serve a practical goal, and the writer has all the time in the world to present his subject as something interesting for its own sake. His characteristic brevity comes from the elegance of his mind, never from pressures of time or employment. The writing is initiated by the writer, not the reader: the writer wants to present something not to a client, but to an indefinite audience, treated as if it were a single individual. His motive is to present truth, not so that someone can use it to accomplish a practical goal, although someone might make use of it for such a purpose, but for its own sake.

3   Classic style and practical style have important areas of overlap; both styles place a high value on clarity and directness. Classic style values clarity because it sees itself as a transparent medium for the presentation of truth. Practical style values clarity because it places a premium on being easy to parse. Both styles can be described as precise and efficient, but for quite different reasons: practical style is precise and efficient because the reader wants to understand well and quickly for the purpose of making immediate use of what he is reading; classic style is precise and efficient because precision serves truth and because efficiency is a refinement. The efficiency of classic style is a sign of its having the leisure and luxury to afford refinement: the writer and reader have had all the time needed to train their minds to the requisite concert pitch.

4   Neither classic style nor practical style contains much of the sort of internal network of cross-references that linguists call "metadiscourse" ("I would like to tell you about x but first I have to tell you about y"). In classic style, such explicit acknowledgment of planning defeats the immediacy and spontaneity that mark the style's model scene, conversation. In practical style, a network of cross-references, clotting the text, is a poor substitute for less distracting indications of coherence.

5   There are a few recognizable prototypes of the model scene of practical style. The first, drawn from the world of corporate business or the legal profession, is a memorandum to a superior who has asked for information. The writer knows more about the subject than the reader, but it is the reader who will make a decision or take action, and so stands in need of some of the writer's knowledge. The reader's need is the motive for writing. A second prototype is a memorandum to a subordinate whose activities the reader is trying to direct and manage. In neither case does the reader want or expect to know everything the writer knows about the subject. Practical style is selective in a way that classic style is not. The cast

is hierarchical, not symmetric. Clustered around these prototypes are recognizable extensions: the manual telling someone how to perform routine jobs; the manual telling someone how to use something; the how-to book instructing the CEO in the art of negotiation; the book about financial planning telling those with discretionary income how to invest it; the advisory from a manufacturer to owners of the manufactured product telling them that it has a defect and how to get it fixed.

6   Another prototype of this scene is the delivery of the results of research to fellow researchers, which is to say, fellow insiders. The writer knows more about his own research than the readers do, but they are fellow professionals who expect to know everything he knows as a result of reading his report, or know at least what they need to know for their own purposes. What is reported will affect their own independent activities in ways that they alone can judge. The writer is imparting information and does not want his writing, as such, to be noticed; it should fulfill every standard expectation and be as easy to parse as possible.

7   Most writing in schools and colleges is a perversion of practical style; the student pretends that he is writing a memorandum. He pretends that he knows more than the reader, that the reader needs this information, and that his job is to impart that information in a way that is easy for the reader to parse. The pretense is supposed to be practice for the real thing. Actually, the reader (the teacher) probably knows more about the subject than the writer; the reader (the teacher) has no need whatever for the information; and the job of the writer is to cover himself from attack by his superior (the teacher). The actual scene interferes so much with the fantasy scene that the result is almost inevitably compromised, if not fraudulent.

Questions

1. How do the authors achieve topic continuity in this passage? How important is this to the passage's overall success?
2. Where and how do the authors use nominalization in the final paragraph? Aside from creating cohesion, how does this nominalization advance the authors' main point in this paragraph?
3. The authors note that conversation is the model scene for classic prose. Can it also be the model scene for practical style? Why or why not? Consider the case of a researcher presenting his (or her) results to colleagues.

Peter Brown

Born in 1935 and educated at Oxford University, Peter Brown is the author of many books on late antiquity and early Christianity, including *Power and Persuasion in Late Antiquity, Augustine of Hippo,* and *The Cult of the Saints.* He has taught history and classics at Oxford and Berkeley, and currently teaches at Princeton University. The following selection is from *The Body and Society: Men, Women, and Sexual Renunciation in Early Christianity* (1988), which investigates early Christian thinking about the body, gender, and holiness.

from *The Body and Society*

1   *I*n the second century A.D., a young man of the privileged classes of the Roman Empire grew up looking at the world from a position of unchallenged dominance. Women, slaves, and barbarians were unalterably different from him and inferior to him. The most obtrusive polarity of all, that between himself and women, was explained to him in terms of a hierarchy based on nature itself. Biologically, the doctors said, males were those fetuses who had realized their full potential. They had amassed a decisive surplus of "heat" and fervent "vital spirit" in the early stages of their coagulation in the womb. The hot ejaculation of male seed proved this: "For it is the semen, when possessed of vitality, which makes us men, hot, well-braced in limbs, heavy, well-voiced, spirited, strong to think and act."

2   Women, by contrast, were failed males. The precious vital heat had not come to them in sufficient quantities in the womb. Their lack of heat made them more soft, more liquid, more clammy-cold, altogether more formless than were men. Periodic menstruation showed that their bodies could not burn up the heavy surpluses that coagulated within them. Yet precisely such surpluses were needed to nurture and contain the hot male seed, thus producing children. Were this not so, the doctor Galen

added, men might think that "the Creator had purposely made one half of the whole race imperfect, and, as it were, mutilated."

3   The sensibilities of a modern reader are understandably bruised by such assertions. We must remember that they had already been made for over half a millennium by this time, and they would continue to be made until this century. They effectively confined women to a lower place than men in an irrefutable, "natural" hierarchy. In the second century, however, the notion was also exploited to subject men themselves to an unremitting process of fine-tuning. Even men could not be entirely sure of themselves. Their superiority to women was not based on a "physiology of incommensurability," such as was elaborated in the nineteenth century, to declare men irrevocably different from women. The medical entities of heat and vital spirit were imponderable elements in the makeup of the male. It could be assumed that men always had more of that precious heat than did women. But this heat, unless actively mobilized, might cool, leading even a man to approach the state of a woman. In the Roman world, the physical appearance and the reputed character of eunuchs acted as constant reminders that the male body was a fearsomely plastic thing. As Galen suggested, in his treatise *On the Seed,* lack of heat from childhood on could cause the male body to collapse back into a state of primary undifferentiation. No normal man might actually become a woman; but each man trembled forever on the brink of becoming "womanish." His flickering heat was an uncertain force. If it was to remain effective, its momentum had to be consciously maintained. It was never enough to be male: a man had to strive to remain "virile." He had to learn to exclude from his character and from the poise and temper of his body all telltale traces of "softness" that might betray, in him, the half-formed state of a woman. The small-town notables of the second century watched each other with hard, clear eyes. They noted a man's walk. They reacted to rhythms of his speech. They listened attentively to the telltale resonance of his voice. Any of these might betray the ominous loss of a hot, high-spirited momentum, a flagging of the clear-cut self-restraint, and a relaxing of the taut elegance of voice and gesture that made a man a man, the unruffled master of a subject world.

Questions

1. Consider Brown's use of such modifiers as "telltale," "ominous," "flickering," and "fearsomely plastic" in the final paragraph. Would you eliminate them? Why or why not?

2. Are the verbs in the final paragraph well chosen? Which ones are most evocative? Do they work well with the modifiers in the same paragraph? Why or why not?
3. Read a paragraph aloud with special attention to sound, rhythm, and sentence variation. Do you hear any false notes? If so, where?
4. Consider the use of the passive voice in the first half of the last paragraph. Would you change any of the passive constructions to active ones? Why or why not?

Margaret Atwood

Born in Nova Scotia in 1939, Margaret Atwood studied literature at the University of Toronto. An accomplished poet, novelist, critic, journalist, and teacher, Atwood also has written for television and radio. "The Female Body" first appeared in *Michigan Quarterly Review* and was anthologized in *The Best American Essays: 1991*. Although the piece resists both practical style and the typical essay form, many of its most potent effects depend on their conventions.

The Female Body

. . . entirely devoted to the subject of "The Female Body." Knowing how well you have written on this topic . . . this capacious topic . . .

—letter from *Michigan Quarterly Review*

1.

1 I agree, it's a hot topic. But only one? Look around, there's a wide range. Take my own, for instance.

2 I get up in the morning. My topic feels like hell. I sprinkle it with water, brush parts of it, rub it with towels, powder it, add lubricant. I dump in the fuel and away goes my topic, my topical topic, my controversial topic, my capacious topic, my limping topic, my nearsighted topic, my topic with back problems, my badly behaved topic, my vulgar topic, my outrageous topic, my aging topic, my topic that is out of the question and anyway still can't spell, in its oversized coat and worn winter boots, scuttling along the sidewalk as if it were flesh and blood, hunting for what's out there, an avocado, an alderman, an adjective, hungry as ever.

2.

3 The basic Female Body comes with the following accessories: garter belt, panti-girdle, crinoline, camisole, bustle, brassiere, stomacher,

chemise, virgin zone, spike heels, nose ring, veil, kid gloves, fish-net stockings, fichu, bandeau, Merry Widow, weepers, chokers, barrettes, bangles, beads, lorgnette, feather boa, basic black, compact, Lycra stretch one-piece with modesty panel, designer peignoir, flannel nightie, lace teddy, bed, head.

3.

4   The Female Body is made of transparent plastic and lights up when you plug it in. You press a button to illuminate the different systems. The circulatory system is red, for the heart and arteries, purple for the veins; the respiratory system is blue; the lymphatic system is yellow; the digestive system is green, with liver and kidneys in aqua. The nerves are done in orange and the brain is pink. The skeleton, as you might expect, is white.

5   The reproductive system is optional, and can be removed. It comes with or without a miniature embryo. Parental judgment can thereby be exercised. We do not wish to frighten or offend.

4.

6   He said, I won't have one of those things in the house. It gives a young girl a false notion of beauty, not to mention anatomy. If a real woman was built like that she'd fall on her face.

7   She said, If we don't let her have one like all the other girls she'll feel singled out. It'll become an issue. She'll long for one and she'll long to turn into one. Repression breeds sublimation. You know that.

8   He said, It's not just the pointy plastic tits, it's the wardrobes. The wardrobes and that stupid male doll, what's his name, the one with the underwear glued on.

9   She said, Better to get it over with when she's young. He said, All right, but don't let me see it.

10   She came whizzing down the stairs, thrown like a dart. She was stark naked. Her hair had been chopped off, her head was turned back to front, she was missing some toes and she'd been tattooed all over her body with purple ink in a scrollwork design. She hit the potted azalea, trembled there for a moment like a botched angel, and fell.

11   He said, I guess we're safe.

5.

12   The Female Body has many uses. It's been used as a door knocker, a bottle opener, as a clock with a ticking belly, as something to hold up lampshades, as a nutcracker, just squeeze the brass legs

together and out comes your nut. It bears torches, lifts victorious wreaths, grows copper wings and raises aloft a ring of neon stars; whole buildings rest on its marble heads.

13   It sells cars, beer, shaving lotion, cigarettes, hard liquor; it sells diet plans and diamonds, and desire in tiny crystal bottles. Is this the face that launched a thousand products? You bet it is, but don't get any funny big ideas, honey, that smile is a dime a dozen.

14   It does not merely sell, it is sold. Money flows into this country or that country, flies in, practically crawls in, suitful after suitful, lured by all those hairless pre-teen legs. Listen, you want to reduce the national debt, don't you? Aren't you patriotic? That's the spirit. That's my girl.

15   She's a natural resource, a renewable one luckily, because those things wear out so quickly. They don't make 'em like they used to. Shoddy goods.

6.

16   One and one equals another one. Pleasure in the female is not a requirement. Pair-bonding is stronger in geese. We're not talking about love, we're talking about biology. That's how we all got here, daughter.

17   Snails do it differently. They're hermaphrodites, and work in threes.

7.

18   Each Female Body contains a female brain. Handy. Makes things work. Stick pins in it and you get amazing results. Old popular songs. Short circuits. Bad dreams.

19   Anyway: each of these brains has two halves. They're joined together by a thick cord; neural pathways flow from one to the other, sparkles of electric information washing to and fro. Like light on waves. Like a conversation. How does a woman know? She listens. She listens in.

20   The male brain, now, that's a different matter. Only a thin connection. Space over here, time over there, music and arithmetic in their own sealed compartments. The right brain doesn't know what the left brain is doing. Good for aiming though, for hitting the target when you pull the trigger. What's the target? Who's the target? Who cares? What matters is hitting it. That's the male brain for you. Objective.

21   This is why men are so sad, why they feel so cut off, why they think of themselves as orphans cast adrift, footloose and stringless in the deep void. What void? she asks. What are you talking about?

The void of the universe, he says, and she says Oh and looks out the window and tries to get a handle on it, but it's no use, there's too much going on, too many rustlings in the leaves, too many voices, so she says, Would you like a cheese sandwich, a piece of cake, and cup of tea? And he grinds his teeth because she doesn't understand, and wanders off, not just alone but Alone, lost in the dark, lost in the skull, searching for the other half, the twin who could complete him.

22   Then it comes to him: he's lost the Female Body! Look, it shines in the gloom, far ahead, a vision of wholeness, ripeness, like a giant melon, like an apple, like a metaphor for "breast" in a bad sex novel; it shines like a balloon, like a foggy noon, a watery moon, shimmering in its egg of light.

23   Catch it. Put it in a pumpkin, in a high tower, in a compound, in a chamber, in a house, in a room. Quick, stick a leash on it, a lock, a chain, some pain, settle it down, so it can never get away from you again.

Questions

1. How and where does Atwood play against the guidelines of clarity, proportion, and relevance? What happens when the guidelines are flouted in this way?

2. Notice the absence of transitions between sentences. What effects are created by this pattern, and what does it suggest about the author's approach to "the topic"?

3. Read section seven aloud. How do the sentences vary over the course of the section? What effects are created by this variation?

4. Compare Atwood's stylistic decisions to Brown's, who also writes about the body. Would his style suit her purpose? Why or why not?

Richard Rorty

Richard Rorty was born in New York City in 1931. He began studying philosophy at the University of Chicago at age 15 and later took a Ph.D. from Yale University. His books on philosophy, politics, and culture include *Philosophy and the Mirror of Nature, Consequences of Pragmatism,* and *Achieving Our Country: Leftist Thought in Twentieth-Century America.* He has taught at Princeton University and the University of Virginia and is currently a professor of comparative literature and philosophy at Stanford University. The following excerpt from "The Intellectuals and the Poor," a speech delivered at Pomona College in February 1996, appeared in the June 1996 issue of *Harper's* magazine.

from *The Intellectuals and the Poor*

1 *I*f one accepts the premise that the basic responsibility of the American left is to protect the poor against the rapacity of the rich, it's difficult to argue that the postwar years have been particularly successful ones. As Karl Marx pointed out, the history of the modern age is the history of class warfare, and in America today, it is a war in which the rich are winning, the poor are losing, and the left, for the most part, is standing by.

2 Early American leftists, from William James to Walt Whitman to Eleanor Roosevelt, seeking to improve the standing of the country's poorest citizens, found their voice in a rhetoric of fraternity, arguing that Americans had a responsibility for the well-being of their fellow man. This argument has been replaced in current leftist discourse by a rhetoric of "rights." The shift has its roots in the fact that the left's one significant postwar triumph was the success of the civil rights movement. The language of "rights" is the language of the documents that have sparked the most successful

attempts to relieve human suffering in postwar America—the series of Supreme Court decisions that began with *Brown v. Board of Education* and continued through *Roe v. Wade*. The Brown decision launched the most successful appeal to the consciences of Americans since the Progressive Era.

3   Yet the trouble with rights talk, as the philosopher Mary Ann Glendon has suggested, is that it makes political morality not a result of political discourse—of reflection, compromise, and choice of the lesser evil—but rather an unconditional moral imperative: a matter of corresponding to something antecedently given, in the way that the will of God or the law of nature is purportedly given. Instead of saying, for example, that the absence of legal protections makes the lives of homosexuals unbearably difficult, that it creates unnecessary human suffering for our fellow Americans, we have come to say that these protections must be instituted in order to protect homosexuals' rights.

4   The difference between an appeal to end suffering and an appeal to rights is the difference between an appeal to fraternity, to fellow-feeling, to sympathetic concern, and an appeal to something that exists quite independently from anybody's feelings about anything—something that issues unconditional commands. Debate about the existence of such commands, and discussion of which rights exist and which do not, seems to me a philosophical blind alley, a pointless importation of legal discourse into politics, and a distraction from what is really needed in this case: an attempt by straights to put themselves in the shoes of the gays.

5   Consider Colin Powell's indignant reaction to the suggestion that the exclusion of gays from the military is analogous to the pre-1950s exclusion of African Americans from the military. Powell angrily insists that there is no analogy here—that gays simply do not have the rights claimed by blacks. As soon as the issue is phrased in rights talk, those who agree with Powell and oppose what they like to call "special rights for homosexuals" start citing the Supreme Court decision in *Bowers v. Hardwick*. The Court looked into the matter and solemnly found that there is no constitutional protection for sodomy. So people arguing against Powell have to contend that *Bowers* was wrongly decided. This leads to an argumentative impasse, one that suggests that rights talk is the wrong approach.

6   The *Brown v. Board of Education* decision was not a discovery of a hitherto unnoticed constitutional right, or of a hitherto unnoticed intention of the authors of constitutional amendments. Rather, it

was the result of our society's long-delayed willingness to admit that the behavior of white Americans toward the descendants of black slaves was, and continued to be, incredibly cruel—that it was intolerable that American citizens should be subjected to the humiliation of segregation. If *Bowers v. Hardwick* is reversed, it will not be because a hitherto invisible right to sodomy has become manifest to the justices. It will be because the heterosexual majority has become more willing to concede that it has been tormenting homosexuals for no better reason than to give itself the sadistic pleasure of humiliating a group designated as inferior—designated as such for no better reason than to give another group a sense of superiority.

7   I may seem to be stretching the term "sadistic," but I do not think I am. It seems reasonable to define "sadism" as the use of persons weaker than ourselves as outlets for our resentments and frustrations, and especially for the infliction of humiliation on such people in order to bolster our own sense of self-worth. All of us have been guilty, at some time in our lives, of this sort of casual, socially accepted sadism. But the most conspicuous instances of sadism, and the only ones relevant to politics, involve groups rather than individuals. Thus Cossacks and the Nazi storm troopers used Jews, and the white races have traditionally used the colored races, in order to bolster their group self-esteem. Men have traditionally humiliated women and beaten up gays in order to exalt their own sense of masculine privilege. The central dynamic behind this kind of sadism is the simple fact that it keeps up the spirits of a lot of desperate, beaten-down people to be able to say to themselves, "At least I'm not a nigger!" or "At least I'm not a faggot!"

8   Sadism, however, is not the only cause of cruelty and needless suffering. There is also selfishness. Selfishness differs from sadism in being more realistic and more thoughtful. It is less a matter of one's self-worth and more a matter of rational calculation. If I own a business and pay my workers more than the minimum necessary to keep them at work, there will be less for me. My paying them less is not sadistic, but it may well be selfish. If I prevent my slaves, or the descendants of my ancestor's slaves, from getting an education, there will be less chance for them to compete with me and my descendants for the good jobs. If suburbanites cast their votes in favor of financing public education through locally administered property taxes, there will be less chance for the children in the cities to be properly educated, and so to compete with

suburban children for membership in a shrinking middle class. All these calculated actions are cruel and selfish, but it would be odd to call them sadistic.

9   Our knowledge of sadism is relatively new—it is something we have only begun to get a grip on with the help of Freud, and philosophers like Sartre and Derrida, who have capitalized on Freud's work. But it is as if the thrill of discovering something new has led us to forget other human impulses; on constant guard against sadism, we have allowed selfishness free reign.

10   Just as rights talk is the wrong approach for issues where appeals to human sympathy are needed, sadism is the wrong target when what is at hand is selfishness. But this is the way American leftists have learned to talk—and think—about the world.

11   You would not guess from listening to the cultural politicians of the academic left that the power of the rich over the poor remains the most obvious, and potentially explosive, example of injustice in contemporary America. For these academics offer ten brilliant unmaskings of unconscious sadism for every unmasking of the selfishness intrinsic to American political and economic institutions. Enormous ingenuity and learning are deployed in demonstrating the complicity of this or that institution, or of some rival cultural politician, with patriarchy or heterosexism or racism. But little gets said about how we might persuade Americans who make more than $50,000 a year to take more notice of the desperate situation of their fellow citizens who make less than $20,000.

12   Instead we hear talk of "the dominant white patriarchal heterosexist culture." This idea isolates the most sadistic patterns of behavior from American history, weaves them together, and baptizes their cause "the dominant culture." It is as if I listed all the shameful things I have ever done in my life and then attributed them to the dark power of "my true, dominant self." This would be a good way to alienate myself from myself, and to induce schizophrenia, but it would not be a good way to improve my behavior. For it does not add anything to the nasty facts about my past to blame them on a specter. Nor does it add anything to the facts about the suffering endured by African Americans and other groups to invent a bogeyman called "the dominant culture."

13   The more we on the American left think that study of psychoanalytic and sociologial or philosophical theory will give us a better grip on what is going on in our country, the less likely we are to speak a political language that will help bring about change in our society. The more we can speak a robust, concrete, and

practical language—one that can be picked up and used by legisla-
tors and judges—the more use we will be.

Questions

1. Consider the sentence: "The Court looked into the matter and
   solemnly found that there is no constitutional protection for
   sodomy." Does the modifier *solemnly* pay its own way? Why
   or why not?
2. The second sentence of the second paragraph uses the passive
   voice: "This argument has been replaced in current leftist discourse by a rhetoric of 'rights'." What, if anything, justifies the
   passive construction at this point in the speech?
3. What is the main topic of paragraph eight? How does Rorty
   develop that topic? Does he sacrifice focus in the process? Why
   or why not?
4. Consider the use of repetition in the last paragraph. What is the
   effect of that repetition?
5. Why does Rorty wish to downplay talk about rights and
   sadism? Why is he so interested in *how* we talk about politics?

William Ian Miller

William Ian Miller is a professor of law at the University of Michigan. Although his work as a legal historian has focused on medieval society and blood feud, his most recent books—*The Anatomy of Disgust, Humiliation,* and *The Mystery of Courage*—explore the emotions of social and moral stratification. "Near Misses" was published in *Michigan Quarterly Review;* an excerpt appeared in the November 1999 issue of *Harper's* magazine.

from *Near Misses*

1   Is it just me or is not a fairly general phenomenon that the almost good looking, the almost witty, the almost cool, are more likely to draw our disapprobation than the plain, the average, the middlingly unassuming? Isn't it the case that "almostness" here registers greater moral and social culpability than the person who sits back in the middle of things? This phenomenon, if I may for the sake of argument assume that it is indeed a phenomenon, plays itself out differently in different domains. Take the case of physical appearance first. There is the erotic allure of a certain kind of imperfection, that sweet disorder in the dress. This style, whether natural or cultivated coyly, is not a near miss at all, but a hit in the domain of Eros. Moreover, the mere signs of sweet disorder seem to work independently of whether they originate in innocent artlessness or in coy contrivance. Contrast the perfect imperfection of sweet disorder with the person who has all the features of beauty but it somehow doesn't add up, or that in a certain slant of light we see not near beauty, something, in other words, that still looks pretty good, but failure, a marring so malignant that we can never see the person, who at first glance attracted us, as attractive again. Sometimes beauty behaves digitally, on or off, rather than on the sliding analogue continuum descending through grades of ever lessening attractiveness. And we blame near misses in the digital ordering of beauty for not measuring up to what we feel they claimed for themselves. So what if they had no choice in the matter? We hold them to have been pretentious, aspiring to be seen as

beautiful and missing in some small, but cancerous, way that brings the whole presumptuous edifice toppling down.

2   So too the almost witty. These people really end up generating annoyance, which annoyance can end up in real loathing. These are Alexander Pope's dunces, or the poetasters of the Elizabethan period, the poser execrated by Johnson and Swift, true men of wit. And likewise the almost cool. The person who just misses ever so slightly the posture, the expression, the scuff of the shoe, the brand of the shirt, the cast of the eye. These people don't quite make it and we hold them culpable, probably rightly so, even as we fear greatly that our monitoring of our own performance may not be quite as astute as our monitoring of others' performances. We may be competent enough in the rules of cool, wit, and beauty, to judge others contemptible as near misses, but we can never be sure we are not being looked at with the same contempt, as having just missed ourselves.

3   What we loathe in these near missing people is the pretense of their thinking that they have hit when they have missed. (Please pardon me for assuming some unidentified "they" are the losers, rather than using "we" here. But in all likelihood a good many of us are some other we's they.) It is the presumption, the self-serving errors of self-perception, that show they think they are doing better than they really are. Now I know I am telling this story in a one-sided rather bleak way, for we all know people so convinced of their own excellence and who carry off their own delusion with such style that they end up charming us and at the same time beating us down with their exuberant and passionate commitment to their inflated self-image, so that our annoyance ends up in a kind of benevolent amusement of admiring disbelief. So they, in fact, end up forcing the world to confirm the rightness of their erroneous judgment of themselves.

4   But let us imagine for instance the perfectly witty and perfectly cool. The witty surely have their bad days. Samuel Johnson, Alexander Pope, and Jane Austen couldn't have been on all the time. But presumably they knew when they were not on, unlike would-be wits who are seldom if ever on and always think they are. Coolness raises different issues. The witty person can withdraw and sit silently or simply engage in conversation that makes no pretense of wit and still maintain his or her deserved reputation as a wit, but the cool must be forever cool. There is no relief. But to be perfectly cool is to raise the suspicion of unnaturalness, having to try too hard. Indeed most all human perfection suggests

unnaturalness. Trees and tigers, in contrast, can be perfect and perfectly natural at the same time, no doubt because we don't quite subject them to moral and sexual demands. The cool person, and perhaps also the person of charm, must have their own sweet disorders in dress and in address too or they seem brittle, contrived, lifeless, and programmed. Perfection in the social order then requires a certain kind of apt imperfection or we suspect sham and pretense. So in the social domain of manners and character, perfection, scoring, hitting it just right, means not always hitting it. But then the not quite hitting must still be just right.

5   This complicates somewhat what it means to miss nearly in the domain of manner and manners. The almost witty person and the almost cool person, the ones who almost make it but who never quite do and who do not have the good sense to bow out of the game end up blowing it, socially and morally, bigger than if they had missed by a mile. For their continuing succession of near misses in fact types them as inept, that is as big missers. Among their many failings, they do not have the competence to see sweet disorderings for the competence they represent, and no doubt they lack the discernment to see why their shortcomings are maybe not so much a function of not getting it right (surely they fail in this conventional way too), but of getting it too right, of looking unnatural, of trying too hard, of not having the confidence and poise of real cool, or the grace of real charm, which allows you to blow it, recover with aplomb, with dignity enhanced. Those almost cool, almost witty people are not really having near misses at all when they miss nearly. The very nearness of their misses, by one measure, is what reveals the complete failure of their expertise in the game at hand. For the game is played out in variations measured by millimicrons and timed in nanoseconds.

6   Not all failure is discrediting. Some provides the opportunity to show poise or to demonstrate that one's failures are the kind that are momentary, not the sort that will forever define one's rank and character downward in the world of honor and esteem. There is another class of failure which is not momentary at all, but rather than lowering honor it raises it: this is the type of failure judged glorious and it is most often associated with heroic defeat. Heroic defeat can make for better stories than heroic victory; heroic losers are often more attractive than heroic winners. The courageous last stand in which the hero stands victorious at the end makes his deeds look suspiciously rational, even prudent, whereas glorious failure suspends rationality, dispenses with prudence and shows unambivalent commitment to grand action and the heroic order.

Yet we would hardly call it a near miss if someone by sheerest accident, meaning to go down fighting, ends up carrying the day just because it is slightly less glorious to survive victoriously than to die nobly. Going down in style is delicately contingent on several key variables that mark the thinnest difference that separates glorious failure from dark comedy. And that thin line of separation puts us squarely in the domain of the near miss.

• • •

7   Bearing some relation to the near miss is the nice try. "Nice try" is what we say to encourage, to keep up the spirits of those trying to acquire reasonable competence in a task they are learning or relearning. But the try still has to measure up to some kind of good-faith standard and even more than good faith is required. There has to be some evidence of an actual skill that is in fact emerging if saying "nice try" is to avoid becoming ironical or brutally sarcastic. You cannot just say "nice try" to any nice try, unless you are one of those souls who believes that people's psyches are so fragile that no matter how inept they are that fact is never to be hinted at.

8   In a more rational order only a very small set of near misses qualify as true nice tries. These are those *grand* efforts that just come up short. The shot rimming out at the buzzer doesn't qualify because the mechanics of taking a basketball shot are not that demanding, but the team coming back from a twenty-point deficit to tie the game with seconds remaining before losing at the buzzer would qualify. Such an effort is a nice try *and* a near miss, which maps on exactly to the other team's narrow escape and close call. But the "nice try" has pretty much been claimed by the world of ridicule and sarcasm. Only parents and physical therapists are more likely to say "nice try" encouragingly than disparagingly; and even then it is hard not to have a tone of exasperation after the second or third "nice try" doesn't yield some genuine improvement in performance. So the nice try comes to signify misses that miss by a mile, but are not so far off that the incompetent bumbler can claim that he wasn't even trying in the first place, that he should, in other words, not be held to account at all. The "nice try" of hostile intent denies to its target any way out. He is simply an inept fool.

• • •

9   What unites the chagrin of the near miss, the relief of the close call, the mortification of the nice try . . . ? With the exception of the nice try, they raise the question of what-if, that there could have been

other outcomes and other paths, if only... But this question is not just experienced as an abstract exercise in the idea of paths not taken or in path dependency itself: it is felt and felt with a powerful amalgam of emotions we have come to understand as "what-if-ness" itself. Miserable as that sense can be at times, it still suggests that we matter, even if only as the object of the gods' laughter. And what of the nice try, the odd man out in this assembly? It works to provide the contrasting term, the ironical negation of the others. Its mode is coddlingly sentimental, denying tragedy, horror, commitment, and suspense, denying, that is, most of the possibility of a good story. Its style is therapeutic in the self-help mold. It's about I'm OK and you're OK, with OK meaning that we passed judgment in a world that makes no demands to be anything but what we already are, that is, it is a world in which what-if is not a possible question. No wonder we use "nice try" to express contempt.

Questions

1. How well does Miller measure information? Identify three passages in which he is especially concerned to achieve the proper level of detail.
2. Consider the transitional phrases in paragraph 4, especially those that signal contrast. What effects do these contrasts produce in this passage? Why might the author wish to create those effects?
3. What is Miller's attitude toward the nice try? How does this attitude relate to the fine discriminations and judgments offered throughout the essay?

Paul Fussell

A decorated Army lieutenant in Wold War II, Paul Fussell was a professor of English at Rutgers University and the University of Pennsylvania, where he taught eighteenth-century British literature. He has written on topics ranging from travel literature to the horrors of modern warfare. His books include *The Great War and Modern Memory*, *Class*, and *Doing Battle*. The following essay is taken from *The Boy Scout Handbook and Other Observations*.

The Boy Scout Handbook

1 **I**t's amazing how many interesting books humanistic criticism manages not to notice. Staring fixedly at its handful of teachable masterpieces, it seems content not to recognize that a vigorous literary-moral life constantly takes place just below (sometimes above) its vision. What a pity Lionel Trilling or Kenneth Burke never paused to examine the intersection of rhetoric and social motive among, say, the Knights of Columbus or the Elks. That these are their fellow citizens is less important than that the desires and rituals of these groups are desires and rituals, and thus of permanent social and psychological consequence. The culture of the Boy Scouts deserves this sort of look-in, especially since the right sort of people don't know much about it.

2 The right sort consists, of course, of liberal intellectuals. They have often gazed uneasily at the Boy Scout movement. After all, a general, the scourge of the Boers, invented it; Kipling admired it; the Hitlerjugend (and the Soviet Pioneers) aped it. If its insistence that there is a God has not sufficed to alienate the enlightened, its khaki uniforms, lanyards, salutes, badges, and flag-worship have seemed to argue incipient militarism, if not outright fascism. The movement has often seemed its own worst enemy. Its appropriation of Norman Rockwell as its official Apelles has not en-

deared it to those of exquisite taste. Nor has its cause been pro-
moted by events like the TV appearance a couple of years ago of
the Chief Pardoner, Gerald Ford, rigged out in a scout neckerchief,
assuring us from the teleprompter that a Scout is Reverent. Then
there are the leers and giggles triggered by the very word "scout-
master," which in knowing circles is alone sufficient to promise
comic pederastic narrative. "*All* scoutmasters are homosexuals,"
asserted George Orwell, who also insisted that "*All* tobacconists
are Fascists."

3   But anyone who imagines that the scouting movement is either
sinister or stupid or funny should spend a few hours with the lat-
est edition of *The Official Boy Scout Handbook* (1979). Social, cultural, and literary historians could attend to it profitably as well, for
after *The Red Cross First Aid Manual, The World Almanac,* and the
Gideon Bible, it is probably the best-known book in this country.
Since the first edition in 1910, twenty-nine million copies have been
read in bed by flashlight. The first printing of this ninth edition is
600,000. We needn't take too seriously the ascription of authorship
to William ("Green Bar Bill") Hillcourt, depicted on the title page
as an elderly gentleman bare-kneed in scout uniform and identified as Author, Naturalist, and World Scouter. He is clearly the Ann
Page or Reddy Kilowatt of the movement, and although he's
doubtless contributed to this handbook (by the same author is
Baden-Powell: The Two Lives of a Hero [1965]), it bears all the marks
of composition by committee, or "task force," as it's called here. But
for all that, it's admirably written. And although a complex sentence is as rare as a reference to girls, the rhetoric of this new edition has made no compromise with what we are told is the new
illiteracy of the young. The book assumes an audience prepared by
a very good high-school education, undaunted by terms like *bios-
phere, ideology,* and *ecosystem.*

4   The pliability and adaptability of the scout movement explains
its remarkable longevity, its capacity to flourish in a world dra-
matically different from its founder's. Like the Roman Catholic
Church, the scout movement knows the difference between cos-
metic and real change, and it happily embraces the one to avoid any
truck with the other. Witness the new American flag patch, now
worn at the top of the right sleeve. It betokens no access of jingo-
ism or threat to a civilized internationalism. It simply conduces to
dignity by imitating a similar affectation of police and fire depart-
ments in anarchic towns like New York City. The message of the
flag patch is not "I am a fascist, straining to become old enough to

purchase and wield guns." It is, rather, "I can be put to quasi-official use, and like a fireman or policeman I am trained in first aid and ready to help."

5   There are other innovations, none of them essential. The breeches of thirty years ago have yielded to trousers, although shorts are still in. The wide-brimmed army field hat of the First World War is a fixture still occasionally seen, but it is now augmented by headwear deriving from succeeding mass patriotic exercises: overseas caps and berets from World War II, and visor caps of the sort worn by General Westmoreland and sunbelt retirees. The scout handclasp has been changed, perhaps because it was discovered in the context of the new internationalism that the former one, in which the little finger was separated from the other three on the right hand, transmitted inappropriate suggestions in the Third World. The handclasp is now the normal civilian one, but given with the left hand. There's now much less emphasis on knots than formerly; as if to signal this change, the neckerchief is no longer religiously knotted at the tips. What used to be known as artificial respiration ("Out goes the bad air, in comes the good") has given way to "rescue breathing." The young are now being familiarized with the metric system. Some bright empiric has discovered that a paste made of meat tenderizer is the best remedy for painful insect stings. Constipation is not the bugbear it was a generation ago. And throughout there is a striking new lyricism. "Feel the wind blowing through your hair," the scout is adjured, just as he is exhorted to perceive that Being Prepared for life means learning "to live happy" and—equally important—"to die happy." There's more emphasis now on fun and less on duty; or rather, duty is validated because, properly viewed, it is a pleasure. (If that sounds like advice useful to grown-ups as well as to sprouts, you're beginning to get the point.)

6   There are only two possible causes of complaint. The term "free world" surfaces too often, although the phrase is mercifully uncapitalized. And the Deism is a bit insistent. The United States is defined as a country "whose people believe in a supreme being." The words "In God We Trust" on the coinage and currency are taken almost as a constitutional injunction. The camper is told to carry along the "Bible, Testament, or prayer book of your faith," even though, for light backpacking, he is advised to leave behind air mattress, knife and fork, and pancake turner. When the scout finds himself lost in the woods, he is to "stay put and have faith that someone will find you." In aid of this end, "Prayer will help." But

the religiosity is so broad that it's harmless. The words "your church" are followed always by the phrase "or synagogue." The writers have done as well as they can considering that they're saddled with the immutable twelve points of Baden-Powell's Scout Law, stating unambiguously that "A Scout is Reverent" and "faithful to his religious duties." But if "You have the right to worship God in your own way," you must see to it that "others retain their right to worship God in their way." Likewise, if "you have the right to speak your mind without fear of prison or punishment," you must "ensure that right for others, even when you do not agree with them." If the book adheres to any politics, they can hardly be described as conservative; they are better described as slightly archaic liberal. It is broadly hinted that industrial corporations are prime threats to clean air and conservation. In every illustration depicting more than three boys, one is black. The section introducing the reader to some Great Americans pays respects not only to Franklin and Edison and John D. Rockefeller and Einstein; it also makes much of Walter Reuther and Samuel Gompers, as well as Harriet Tubman, Martin Luther King, and Whitney Young. There is a post-Watergate awareness that public officials must be watched closely. One's civic duties include the obligation to "keep up on what is going on around you" in order to "get involved" and "help change things that are not good."

7 Few books these days could be called compendia of good sense. This is one such, and its good sense is not merely about swimming safely and putting campfires "cold out." The good sense is psychological and ethical as well. Indeed, this handbook is among the very few remaining popular repositories of something like classical ethics, deriving from Artistotle and Cicero. Except for the handbook's adhesions to the motif of scenic beauty, it reads as if the Romantic movement had never taken place. The constant moral theme is the inestimable benefits of looking objectively outward and losing consciousness of self in the work to be done. To its young audience vulnerable to invitations to "trips" and trances and anxious self-absorption, the book calmly says: "Forget yourself." What a shame the psychobabblers of Marin County will never read it.

8 There is other invaluable advice, applicable to adults as well as to scouts. Some is practical, like "Never use flammable fluids to start a charcoal fire. They burn off fast, lighting only a little of the charcoal." Some is civic-moral: "Take a 2-hour walk where you live. Make a list of things that please you, another of things that should be improved." And the the kicker: "Set out to improve

them." Some advice is even intellectual, and pleasantly uncompromising: "Reading trash all the time makes it impossible for anyone to be anything but a second-rate person." But the best advice is ethical: "Learn to think." "Gather knowledge." "Have initiative." "Respect the rights of others." Actually, there's hardly a better gauge for measuring the gross official misbehavior of the seventies than the ethics enshrined in this handbook. From its explicit ethics you can infer such propositions as "A scout does not tap his acquaintances' telephones," or "A scout does not bomb and invade a neutral country, and then lie about it," or "A scout does not prosecute war unless, as the Constitution provides, it has been declared by the Congress." Not to mention that because a scout is clean in thought, word, and deed, he does not, like Richard Nixon, designate his fellow citizens "shits" and then both record his filth and lie about the recordings ("A scout tells the truth").

9 　　Responding to Orwell's satiric analysis of "Boys' Weeklies" forty years ago, the boys' author Frank Richards, stigmatized by Orwell as a manufacturer of excessively optimistic and falsely wholesome stories, observed that "The writer for young people should . . . endeavor to give his young readers a sense of stability and solid security, because it is good for them, and makes for happiness and peace of mind." Even if it is true, as Orwell objects, that the happiness of youth is a cruel delusion, then, says Richards, "Let youth be happy, or as happy as possible. Happiness is the best preparation for misery, if misery must come. At least the poor kid will have had something." In the current world of Making It and Getting Away with It, there are not many books devoted to associating happiness with virtue. The shelves of the CIA and the State Department must be bare of them. "Horror swells around us like an oil spill," Terrence Des Pres said recently. "Not a day passes without more savagery and harm." He was commenting on Philip Hallie's *Lest Innocent Blood Be Shed,* an account of a whole French village's trustworthiness, loyalty, helpfulness, friendliness, courtesy, kindness, cheerfulness, and bravery in hiding scores of Jews during the Occupation. Des Pres concludes: "*Goodness.* When was the last time anyone used that word in earnest, without irony, as anything more than a doubtful cliché?" *The Official Boy Scout Handbook,* for all its focus on Axmanship, Backpacking, Cooking, First Aid, Flowers, Hiking, Map and Compass, Semaphore, Trees, and Weather, is another book about goodness. No home, and certainly no government office, should be without a copy. The generously low price of $3.50 is enticing, and so is the place on the back cover where you're invited to inscribe your name.

Questions

1. What sort of audience does Fussell have in mind? Does he assume any interest among that audience in *The Boy Scout Handbook*? Is this a realistic assumption?
2. Read a paragraph aloud and with emphasis. Where does the stress within the sentences tend to fall?
3. Why are there so few transitional modifiers? Does this result in awkward transitions? Why or why not?
4. How would you describe the tone of this piece? Where is this tone most noticeable? Which stylistic decisions account for it?

Carol J. Clover

Carol Clover is a professor of Scandinavian and rhetoric at the University of California, Berkeley, where she also earned her doctoral degree. Although most of her scholarship focuses on Icelandic family saga, her most acclaimed work to date analyzes gender in a more notorious genre: the modern horror film. The claims in this excerpt are later superceded, but the passage offers a distinctive example of academic writing.

from *Men, Women, and Chainsaws: Gender in the Modern Horror Film*

1   A figurative and functional analysis of the slasher begins with the processes of point of view and identification. The male viewer seeking a male character, even a vicious one, with whom to identify in a sustained way has little to hang onto in the standard example. On the good side, the only viable candidates are the boyfriends or schoolmates of the girls. They are for the most part marginal, undeveloped characters. More to the point, they tend to die early in the film. If the traditional horror plot gave the male spectator a last-minute hero with whom to identify, thereby "indulging his vanity as protector of the helpless female," the slasher eliminates or accentuates that role beyond any such function; indeed, would-be rescuers are not infrequently blown away for their trouble, leaving the girl to fight her own fight. Policemen, father, and sheriffs appear only long enough to demonstrate risible incomprehension and incompetence. On the bad side, there is the

killer. The killer is often unseen or barely glimpsed, during the first part of the film, and what we do see, when we finally get a good look, hardly invites immediate or conscious empathy. He is commonly masked, fat, deformed, or dressed as a woman. Or "he" *is* a woman: woe to the viewer of *Friday the Thirteenth I* who identifies with the male killer only to discover, in the film's final sequences, that he was not a man at all but a middle-aged mother. In either case, the killer is himself eventually killed or otherwise evacuated from the narrative. No male character of any stature lives to tell the tale.

2 The one character of stature who does live to tell the tale is in fact the Final Girl. She is introduced at the beginning and is the only character to be developed in any psychological detail. We understand immediately from the attention paid it that hers is the main story line. She is intelligent, watchful, levelheaded; the first character to sense something amiss and the only one to deduce from the accumulating evidence the pattern and extent of the threat; the only one, in other words, whose perspective approaches our own privileged understanding of the situation. We register horror as she stumbles on the corpses of her friends. Her momentary paralysis in the face of death duplicates those moments of the universal nightmare experience—in which she is the undisputed "I"—on which horror frankly trades. When she downs the killer, we are triumphant. She is by any measure the slasher film's hero. This is not to say that our attachment to her is exclusive and unremitting, only that it adds up, and that in the closing sequence (which can be quite prolonged) it is very close to absolute.

3 An analysis of the camerawork bears this out. Much is made of the use of the I-camera to represent the killer's point of view. In these passages—they are usually few and brief, but striking—we see through his eyes and (on the soundtrack) hear his breathing and heartbeat. His and our vision is partly obscured by the bushes or window blinds in the foreground. By such means we are forced, the logic goes, to identify with the killer . . . We are linked, in this way, with the killer in the early part of the film, usually before we have seen him directly and before we have come to know the Final Girl in any detail. Our closeness to him wanes as our closeness to the Final Girl waxes—a shift underwritten by story line as well as camera position. By the end, point of view is hers: we are in the closet with her, watching with her eyes the knife blade pierce the door; in the room, with her as the killer breaks through the window and grabs at her; in the car with her as the killer stabs through the convertible roof, and so on. And with her, we become

if not the killer of the killer then the agent of his expulsion from the narrative vision. If, during the film's course, we shifted our sympathies back and forth and dealt them out to other characters along the way, we belong in the end to the Final Girl; there is no alternative. When Stretch eviscerates Chop Top at the end of *Texas Chain Saw II*, she is literally the only character left alive, on either side.

• • •

4 The slasher is hardly the first genre in the literary and visual arts to invite identification with the female; one cannot help wondering more generally whether the historical maintenance of images of women in fear and pain does not have more to do with male vicarism than is commonly acknowledged. What distinguishes the slasher, however, is the absence or untenability of alternative perspectives and hence the exposed quality of the invitation . . . The fact that masculine males (boyfriends, father, would-be rescuers) are regularly dismissed through ridicule or death or both would seem to suggest that it is not masculinity per se that is being privileged, but masculinity in conjunction with a female body—indeed, as the victim-hero contemplates, masculinity in conjunction with femininity. For if "masculine" describes the Final Girl some of the time, and in some of her more theatrical moments, it does not do justice to the sense of her character as a whole. She alternates between registers from the outset; before her final struggle she endures the deepest throes of "femininity"; and even during the final struggle she is now weak and now strong, now flees the killer and now charges him, now stabs and is stabbed, now cries out in fear and now shouts in anger. She is a physical female and characterological androgyne: like her name, not masculine but either/or, both, ambiguous.

Questions

1. Read paragraph 3 or 4 aloud, paying special attention to rhythm, sound, variety, and emphasis. Does the repetition help or hinder Clover's effort to develop her main points?
2. Review the first and final sentences of each paragraph. Is it clear where the paragraphs are going and what their main points are?
3. Consider the pronoun choices (in paragraph 2 and elsewhere), especially the use of the first person plural *we*. How does this choice relate to Clover's argument about point of view and identification?

Sample Answers to Selected Exercises

Because style is always a matter of choice, your answers may differ from the ones given here. If so, try to determine how and why your answers are preferable to these.

Exercise 2.1

1. The diaries depict the hypocrisy of that period.
2. The memorandum implies that what happened was proper.
3. His fear of failure hindered his relationship with his son.
4. This film successfully documents the excitement of a political campaign.
5. They concluded that the results were invalid.
6. The experiences transform him into a thoughtful adult.
7. She obviously desires a healthy, balanced relationship.
8. There's no need to establish protocols for these cases.
9. The need for charity varies across cities and states.
10. The research presented in this report focuses on the relationship between residents and their elected officials.

Exercise 3.1

1. Life in all of its complexity imitates *art*.
2. She endured *slander* and *calumny* over her forty-year career.
3. Did you order the *tickets* for the show on Friday night?
4. In a long and sometimes rambling harangue, he cited several failed *policies*.
5. His principal argument challenges commonsense *understandings* of what is known to economists as the fallacy of composition.

Exercise 3.3

1. It's difficult to find many similarities between James Brown and Beck.
2. The Victorian class system tolerated and perpetuated cruelty.
3. Case studies of marketing mistakes prompted a thorough review of competition among brewers.
4. International aid groups had little success after the diplomats withdrew from the capital.
5. Both a hospital's profit status and its affiliation with or ownership by a multi-hospital corporation may affect its organization, service provision, costs, and access to or quality of care.

Exercise 4.1

1. Advertising has been used with great success by politicians.
2. Local parents reported ten cases of measles.
3. Proponents of the plan have advanced several arguments.
4. Ninety percent of the current work force was hired by the company between 1980 and 1985.
5. The committee investigated the charges and found them to be false.

Exercise 4.3

1. In such cases, the defendant's right to remain silent cannot be abridged, even if that silence endangers another officer.
2. When you're dealing with attorneys of that kind, be careful not to arouse their suspicions.
3. This rhetorical strategy flatters readers by making them part of the solution to the problem under consideration.

Exercise 5.1

1. In its day, this novel was considered *somewhat obscene*. (offensive, indecent, lewd)
2. The coach was *to a certain extent happy* with the team's performance. (satisfied, pleased)
3. Although she scandalized most critics, audiences across the country found her *extremely humorous*. (hilarious)
4. There was something *rather vulgar* about the circus-like atmosphere of the trial. (unseemly, shabby, tawdry)

5. The witness appeared to be *totally mixed up* by the line of questioning. (baffled, bewildered, perplexed)

Exercise 5.2

1. The protagonist is a fascinating character.
2. There are many significant parallels between this case and the previous one.
3. Many Americans believe that the boy should not be turned over to his father. There are sound reasons for this judgment, but the risk the mother took on behalf of herself and her son speaks volumes. I believe the father does not want his son so much as a foreign tyrant wants to claim a possession.
4. The local population seems to regard blood-feud as important. Some do not regard chronic low-level violence as out of place, and the informant probably approved of vendetta as well. I will limit myself to the most relevant episode he mentioned during our interviews.

Exercise 5.3

1. It almost seems that the author of "Man Seeking Woman" asked women what they wanted and wrote his ad accordingly. He comes off as insecure.
2. I am very interested in the ESL position and Wilson High School and believe that my coursework has prepared me well for it.
3. There is a widespread debate in this country over the legalization of marijuana. Some people believe that it should remain illegal because its effects are detrimental. Some even believe that it causes insanity.
4. I believe it is in society's best interest to legalize drugs. Although legalization may present certain risks to society, these risks are worth taking. Most law enforcement officials believe that their efforts do not reduce drug abuse significantly in the United States or internationally.
5. The Trojan war appears to be revenge for Helen's abduction. However, the poet concentrates far too much on plunder for revenge to be the only motive. Homer's account was probably shaped more by the demands of narrative than by actual events.

Exercise 6.1

1. In June, management decided that the entire line needed a new advertising campaign. This *decision* was supported by the July sales figures.
2. The new immigrants prospered for the next several decades. Their *prosperity* has been attributed to a number of factors.
3. The national leaders perceived a shift in the public's attitude and revised their plans accordingly. At the local level, however, many observers argued that this *perception* was inaccurate.
4. Trade and production continued to deteriorate as a result of these policies. The empire was locked in a vicious circle, in which responses to this *deterioration* diminished the chances of recovery.
5. This most recent book, for example, omits any mention of research conducted in the last fifteen years. The *omission* is all the more unusual given the author's stated goal of evaluating the effects of this research on current practice.

Exercise 6.3

1. Although action movies are very popular now, I don't like them because they seem more interested in explosions and car chases than in character and plot. In *Cliffhanger*, for example, the director seems to put all his creative energy into the opening sequence.
2. The linguist was struck by the man's speech patterns, which were characteristic of the local dialect. Even so, she had little interest in him as a person. When he asked her to be his teacher, however, her curiosity was aroused.
3. Most of the poem's many critics agree that religion is a major theme. Although religion clearly is important, other themes are even more central.

Glossary
of Terms

The following definitions are meant to be handy rather than complete, authoritative, or watertight. Some of the terms resist precise explanation, while others vary from one grammatical theory to the next. Even so, these definitions should help you understand key concepts in this book and follow other discussions of English grammar and style. Both the definitions and examples frequently supplement those offered in the text; to locate those, consult the Index.

Active Voice.   The regular or unmarked form of a sentence with a transitive verb in which the subject is generally the agent. Contrasts with the passive voice.

> Active: The officer *arrested* Chris.

> Passive: Chris *was arrested.*

Adjective.   A word used to modify nouns, pronouns, and other nounlike elements.

> *white* house, *smaller* dog, *graceful* exit.

Adverb.   A word that modifies a verb by adding information about such things as time and manner. Often ends in *-ly*.

> They turned *around* and ran *over* to the window.

> We went to the zoo *yesterday.*

> They sang *beautifully.*

> I recited the alphabet *backward.*

Agent.   The initiator or source of an action. Usually the subject of a sentence in the active voice.

> *My friends* threw a party.

Alliteration.   The repetition of sound.

> *p*ride of *p*lace, *d*eputy *d*ogcatcher

Antecedent.   The noun or noun-equivalent to which a pronoun refers.

Aspect. A feature of the verb phrase that indicates whether an action is seen as complete or incomplete, or as beginning, ending, continuing, or repeating. Not to be confused with tense, which indicates when something happened. The following sentences are all in the past tense but express different aspects:

I did the crossword puzzle. (perfective)

I was doing the crossword puzzle. (imperfective/progressive)

I had done the crossword puzzle. (perfect)

I used to do the crossword puzzle. (habitual)

Auxiliary Verb. A helping verb that either modifies the main verb or serves as a placeholder in a larger construction.

It *may* rain.	It *will* rain.
I *have* eaten lunch.	*Did* you eat lunch?
I *did* not eat.	Chris *was* elected.
They *are* going home.	

Clause. A structured group of words with a subject and a verb.

I laugh/laughed	if I laugh/laughed
when I laugh/laughed	that I laugh/laughed
because I was laughing	

Independent (or main) clauses stand as complete sentences by themselves.

I laughed

I was laughing

Dependent (or subordinate) clauses must be attached to an independent clause in order to form a complete sentence.

I was thinking of you *when I laughed.*

If I laughed at the wrong time, I apologize.

Cohesion. What holds a text together: more specifically, the grammatical, semantic, and pragmatic connections within a text, and that define it as a text. Produced by given information, pronouns and their antecedents, and other grammatical, logical, temporal, and pragmatic links between sentences and paragraphs.

Complement. A word, phrase, or clause that completes the meaning of a verb.

I bought *the car.*

She seems *tired.*

We stuck *the sandwich in the basket.*

He thought *we were crazy.*

Connotation.   An association or secondary meaning generated by a word. Contrasts with denotation.

Denotation.   The primary, literal, or "dictionary" meaning of a word.

Diction.   The choice of words.

Direct Object.   A noun phrase or nounlike element that is acted on or receives the action of a transitive verb.

She hit *the ball.*   I pet *the puppy.*

The direct object is distinguished from the *indirect object.*

She hit the ball to *Kerry.*   I bought the puppy from *Chris.*

Discourse Marker.   A word or phrase that denotes little or nothing by itself but that signals the relationship between a sentence and the discourse as a whole. *See* Index.

Gerund.   A verb form ending in -ing that functions as a noun.

Voting is important.

Complaining doesn't help.

Given (or Known) Information.   Information that a writer or speaker assumes is already known to the audience. Often appears in the subject slot of a sentence. Contrasts with *new information,* which a writer or speaker assumes is not already known, and which normally appears in the predicate.

Grammar.   A body of rules, conventions, and generalizations that constitute or describe a language.

Imperative Mood.   The command form of a verb.

Stop the presses.   Please *pass* the salt.

The imperative contrasts with the indicative and subjunctive moods. In general, imperative sentences are meant to get the state of affairs in the world to match our words.

Indicative mood.   The assertive form of a verb.

> I *stopped* the presses.   I always *pass* the salt.

In general, indicative sentences are meant to get our words to match the state of affairs in the world. As such, and in contrast to sentences in the imperative and subjunctive moods, most indicative sentences can be said to be true or false.

Indirect Object.   *See* Direct Object.

Intransitive Verb.   A verb that, when combined with a subject, forms a complete thought.

> The spectators *wept.*   The team *rallied.*
>
> I *showered.*   The audience *laughed.*

Metaphor.   An implied and figurative comparison between two distinctly different things.

> The new marketing plan fell flat.
>
> We pitched the idea last week.

Modifier.   A word, phrase, or clause that limits, specifies, or describes another element.

> the *dark* night
>
> *Before you object,* let me explain.
>
> The argument is, *to my way of thinking,* absurd.
>
> They looked at me *suspiciously.*

Mood.   A category of the verb that indicates the manner of representation. Mood is used to assert or record states of affairs in the world (indicative), to command (imperative mood), or to offer a blueprint for possible, desirable, or counterfactual states of affairs (subjunctive).

> God blesses America.   (indicative)
>
> God, bless America!   (imperative)
>
> God bless America.   (subjunctive)

Modal Auxiliary.   A helping verb that expresses necessity, possibility, permission, obligation, or volition. The English modal auxiliaries and their past forms are *shall/should, will/would, may/might, can/could,* and *must.* (Some linguists include *have to, ought to, need to, seem to, happen to,* and *dare to* in this class.)

New Information.　*See* Given Information.

Nominalization.　Producing a noun from another part of speech.

manipulate → manipulation　　occur → occurrence

happy → happiness　　　　　　true → truth

Noun.　A word that typically refers to a person, place, or thing. Most nouns can be inflected for number and possession (man/ men/man's), and many have characteristic endings.

produc*tion*, enjoy*ment*, free*dom*, heal*th*, ripe*ness*

Passive Voice.　A sentence in which a form of *be* is combined with a past participle, and in which the direct object of a transitive verb appears in the subject slot.

The meeting *was cancelled.*

The photograph *was discovered* after the election.

Past Participle.　A verb form often identical to the past tense, but that frequently functions as a modifier: *chapped* lips, *broken* windows. Follows forms of *have* and *be* in perfect and passive constructions.

The transistor was *invented* after the war.

I haven't *attended* class for over two weeks.

They had *driven* over two hundred miles that day.

Perfect.　A construction with a form of *have* plus the past participle.

Present perfect: They *have seen* it.

Past perfect (or pluperfect): They *had seen* it.

Phrase.　A word or group of words that forms a unit of a sentence. Examples include noun phrases, verb phrases, adjective phrases, and prepositional phrases.

Pragmatics.　A sub-field of linguistics that focuses on how speakers do things with language. Distinct from grammar, which is concerned with the internal structure of language.

Predicate.　The part of the sentence that comments on the subject. Includes everything but the subject, which it usually follows.

Dana *brought the paintings all the way from Los Angeles.*

Right now, millions of spectators *are watching on television.*

Preposition. A word that precedes a noun or noun phrase, and that usually designates position, direction, or means.

at, by, of, from, with, against

Prepositional Phrase. A preposition along with its object , usually a noun phrase (sometimes called the object of a preposition).

behind the garage, from Hong Kong, without a clue

Present Participle. A verb form ending in -ing which often functions as a modifier: *billowing* sails, *bulging* deficits. Follows forms of *be* in progressive constructions.

We were *watching* the whole thing on television.

They're *leaving* town tomorrow.

Present participles are distinct from *gerunds,* which also end in -ing but function as nouns.

Timing is everything.

Writing is fun.

Progressive. A verb phrase with a form of *be* followed by a present participle. Usually used to describe ongoing or incomplete activity. *See* Present Participle.

Pronoun. A word that substitutes for a noun or nounlike element.

When *I* left, *they* were still here.

Rhetoric. The study of effective writing or speech.

Semantics. The study of linguistic meaning, especially the meaning of words, phrases, and sentences.

Subject. The first noun phrase or nounlike element in a sentence. Usually functions as the topic of its sentence.

Subjunctive Mood. *See* Mood.

Syntax. The arrangement of words and phrases in sentences.

Tense. A category of the verb that encodes location in time. There are two grammatical tenses in English, past and present.

Present: The earth revolve*s* around the sun.

Past: The earth revolv*ed* around the sun.

Can be combined with auxiliaries to refer to other time frames.

> I *may/will/shall* be there. (present tense, refers to future)
>
> I *had* been waiting. (past perfect or pluperfect)

Tone.   An implicit attitude toward the topic conveyed by writers through their stylistic choices.

Topic.   What a sentence comments on. Usually but not always the grammatical subject of the sentence.

> *Protectionism* is becoming popular again.
>
> Many officials think a *trade war* is likely.

Transitive Verb.   A verb that requires at least one complement.

> I *admire* my aunt.
>
> She *composed* the entire letter in ten minutes.

Transitional Phrase.   A word or phrase that signals the relationship between sentences.

Verb.   A word with identifiable grammatical features that usually expresses action or being. Verbs can be marked for tense and combined with auxiliary verbs. Main verbs agree with the subject in number. Some have characteristic endings: regu*late*, lega*lize*, magn*ify*.

Verb Phrase.   A verb together with its complements and modifiers.

Voice.   A feature of the verb phrase that frames the relationship between characters, things, and events. *See* Active Voice, Passive Voice.

Credits

Index

Abstraction, 8, 23
Active voice, 19–24, 101
Adjective, 30, 101
Adverb, 101
Agent, 20, 101
Alliteration, 49, 101
Alphabetic literacy. *See*
    literacy.
Antecedent, 42-44
Anti-paragraph, 38-39
Aspect, 102
Atwood, Margaret. *See*
    "Female Body, The."
Audience, 5, 20-21, 24, 31-32,
    37, 39, 41, 50
Auxiliary verb, 29, 102

Body and Society, The (Peter
    Brown), 70-72
"Boy Scout Handbook, The"
    (Paul Fussell), 87-92
Brown, Peter. *See Body and
    Society, The.*

Characters, 19
Clarity, 3, 8, 23-24, 37
Classic style, 40, 68-69

Clause, 102
Clear and Simple as the Truth
    (Francis-Noël Thomas and
    Mark Turner), 67-69
Clover, Carol J. See "Men,
    Women, and Chainsaws."
Cohesion, 38-46, 102
Colloquialism, 29-30
Complement, 12-16, 102
Connotation, 103
Conversation, 1-4, 29-30, 37,
    39, 44-45
Conversational guidelines, 2-4,
    15, 34
    See also relevance, proportion,
    clarity.
Cooperation, 1, 21
Crews, Frederick, 45

Denotation, 103
Development, 38-39
Diction, 29-30, 103
Direct object, 11, 20, 103
Discourse marker, 44, 103

Economy, 12-16
Emphasis, 47-49, 51-52

111

"Female Body, The" (Margaret Atwood), 73–76
Focus, 38–39
Fussell, Paul. *See* "Boy Scout Handbook, The."

Gender, 27
Given information, 39-41, 103
Grammar, 103
Grice, H.P., x

Hedging, 30-34

Imperative mood, 103
Indicative mood, 104
Indirect object, 11, 104
"Intellectuals and the Poor, The" (Richard Rorty), 77-81
Intransitive verb, 12

Linguistics, x
Literacy, ix
Logic, xi

Measuring information. *See* proportion.
Metadiscourse, 68
Metaphor, 60-62, 104
"Men, Women, and Chainsaws" (Carol J. Clover), 93-95
Miller, William Ian. *See* "Near Misses."
Modal auxiliary, 29, 104
Modifier, 12-16, 32, 104
    Excessive modification, 15, 33
Mood, 104

See also indicative, imperative, subjunctive
Morris, William, 52

"Near Misses" (William Ian Miller), 82-86
New information, 39-41, 51-52, 105
Nominalization, 41-42, 105
Noun, 105

Overstating the claim, 31-32

Passive voice, 20, 105
Past participle, 105
Perfect, 105
    See also aspect.
Personal ads, 64-66
Plain style, 39-40
Pluperfect, 105
Practical style, 5, 67-69
Pragmatics, x
Predicate, 105
Preposition, 51, 106
Prepositional phrase, 106
Present participle, 106
Pretentious style, 3
Progressive, 106
    See also aspect.
Pronoun, 106
    Pronoun choice, 26-27
Proportion, 2, 22-23, 27

Redundancy, 13-14
Relevance, 3, 21-22
Renoir, Jean, 31, 46
Repetition, 48-49
Revision, 7
    For clarity and economy, 12-16, 29-34

For cohesion, 37-46
For depth and support, 55-62
For variety, 47-52
Rhetoric, 106
Rhythm, 47-49
Rorty, Richard. *See* "Intellectuals and the Poor, The."

Scientific writing, 19
Semantics, 106
Slowing down, 56-58
Smothering the claim, 33
Streamlining, 9
Strong endings, 50-52
Style
  preconceptions about, 4-5
  "rules" of, 2, 26
  See also practical style.
Subject, 20, 106
Syntax, 106

Tense, 106
Thomas, Francis-Noël, 39-41
  See also Clear and Simple as the Truth.
Throat-clearing, 30-31
Tone, 107
Topic, 107
Topic continuity, 23, 25
Transitions, 44-46
Transitive verb, 11, 107
Turn-taking, 37
Turner, Mark, 39-41
  See also Clear and Simple as the Truth.

Vagueness, 29
Variety, 47-50
Verb, 107
Verb phrase, 107
Verb selection, 7-9, 25

Voice, 19-24, 107
  See also active voice, passive voice.

Writing
  As action, x
  As process, 7-9, 37, 58-62
  As technology, ix
  For the Web, 5